pray

TH1NK
™

Go   Ahead :

TH1NK: *about God*

about life

about others

Faith isn't just an act; it's something you live—something huge and sometimes unimaginable. By getting into the real issues in your life, TH1NK books open opportunities to talk honestly about your faith, your relationship with God and others, as well as all the things life throws at you.

Don't let other people th1nk for you . . .

TH1NK for yourself.

www.th1nkbooks.com

pray

by Tony Jones

TH1NK Books
an imprint of NavPress®

NAVPRESS
P.O. Box 35001
Colorado Springs, CO 80935

The Navigators is an international Christian organization. Our mission is to reach, disciple, and equip
people to know Christ and to make Him known through successive generations. We envision multitudes
of diverse people in the United States and every other nation who have a passionate love for Christ, live
a lifestyle of sharing Christ's love, and multiply spiritual laborers among those without Christ.

NavPress is the publishing ministry of The Navigators. NavPress publications help believers learn biblical truth and apply what they learn to their lives and ministries. Our mission is to stimulate spiritual
formation among our readers.

ISBN 1-57683-452-2

Cover and interior design: BURNKIT
Creative Team: Jay Howver, Vicki Newby, Nat Akin, Darla Hightower, Glynese Northam

Some of the anecdotal illustrations in this book are true to life and are included with the permission of
the persons involved. All other illustrations are composites of real situations, and any resemblance to
people living or dead is coincidental.

CIP Data Applied For

Printed in Canada

1 2 3 4 5 6 7 8 9 10 / 07 06 05 04 03

FOR A FREE CATALOG OF
NAVPRESS BOOKS & BIBLE STUDIES,
CALL 1-800-366-7788 (USA)
OR 1-416-499-4615 (CANADA)

CONTENTS

PREFACE

This book, from conception to completion, has been good for my spirit, good for my soul, and good for my life. I've taken a journey through Christian prayer, starting with the pre-Christian prayers of our Israelite forefathers and coming right up to the present day.

I have enjoyed the process from beginning to end, especially seeing how approaches to God and reasons for approaching God are similar from person to person: We're created beings, we desire relationships with our Creator, thus we pray.

My prayer life has been enhanced as a result of this experience. I pray your prayer life will be enhanced by reading this book and putting its ideas into practice.

My deepest thanks go to my wife, Julie, my partner in everything; our children, Tanner and Lily; and Jay and Jen Howver at NavPress.

PART ONE

INTRODUCTION

CHAPTER ONE

WHAT IS PRAYER?

We've all had those moments when we've called out to God in prayers so heartfelt and desperate that the prayer was truly the cry of the heart. I've had many such moments in my life. Some turned out to be fairly silly—I wasn't in the bind I thought I was—and others have been frightening moments into which God intervened.

Somewhere between the points of silly and frightening is an experience I remember vividly. I was skiing at Winter Park Ski Resort in Colorado during seventh grade. I spent the morning skiing with my dad and brother, even though my ability wasn't quite up to theirs. After they were sufficiently warmed up and stretched out, they were feeling bold. I was just trying to keep up and not show my nervousness.

We boarded the Olympia Express chair lift and chatted on our way up. At the top, we jumped off the lift, me following my dad and brother. We skied through a narrow opening in a snow fence and past a sign labeled "Drunken Frenchman." A black diamond, the international symbol indicating that the difficulty of the slope requires expert skiing, was printed on it. Another sign featured smaller print saying something about danger and the required length for skis and the words *at your own risk,* but I didn't take the time to read it.

On a crest along the top of the run, I looked down. I almost puked. The ski run appeared to go straight down, with moguls as tall as I was. My brother went over the edge with no hesitation, carving his way between the bumps. I, on the other hand, stood paralyzed. My skin began to prickle in the same way it does when your foot falls asleep — but it was happening over my entire body. Sweat started dripping from my armpits down my sides. I could feel it. The lump in my throat was too big for me to talk. I had every physical symptom of terror.

My dad must have sensed my anxiety because he asked if we should take off our skis and hike back to the lift in search of another run. When I turned around, I realized getting back would take an hour-long climb. Between that and the fact that my brother would be waiting for us at the bottom, I knew turning around wasn't an option. My dad said he would go first, slowly, so I could follow his path. And he started down.

It was then, standing on that mountain, looking down at certain death — or at least many broken bones — that I uttered a prayer of profound theological depth: "O God, please, please, please, please, help me to ski this and not be permanently injured." Knowing I was in deep trouble, I cried out to God, like the psalmist:

> *Help, GOD—the bottom has fallen out of my life!*
> *Master, hear my cry for help!*
> *Listen hard! Open your ears!*
> *Listen to my cries for mercy.* (Psalm 130:1-2)

I didn't know what else to do except pray. I prayed—and begged and pleaded—that God would give me the strength to do something I couldn't do on my own. Then I started down Drunken Frenchman. As you might guess, I lived to tell about it. I'm here today, still skiing and still praying—and still talking to my dad and brother.

I'm deeply comforted knowing God heard my prayer and cared enough about me, standing at the top of a black-diamond run, to take pity on my situation. The fact that the God of the universe takes personal interest in each of us as we converse with him through prayer is one of the most beautiful aspects of being a follower of Christ.

OUR WORKING DEFINITION

Probably, when most of us think of prayer, we think of asking God for something. Indeed, the word *prayer* means the act of asking for something from God. Most of us will agree with a richer definition of prayer than simply asking for things, though.

Luis of Granada, a sixteenth-century Christian spiritual writer from Spain, wrote, "Prayer, properly speaking, is a petition which we make to God for the things which pertain to our salvation; but it is also taken in another, broader sense to mean any raising of the heart to God."[1] He makes a good point. While we often think of prayer as *asking*, and we most often *ask* when we pray, prayer is actually any time we converse with God—so we may be thanking him, praising him, pouring out our hearts to him, or even sitting in silence before him.

The apostle Paul, in two letters—Philippians 4:6 and 1 Thessalonians 5:17—told us to pray always. Because we do a lot more than think about how much we want things and need things as we go about our days, Paul must have meant that we should be in constant contact with God about what's going on in our lives, our minds, and our souls.

While you're reading this book, we'll consider this to be our working definition of prayer:

Prayer is the act of conversing with God.

Whenever we're in conversation with God, we're at prayer, whether we're in church reciting the Lord's Prayer, going around the circle in youth group, driving in our cars, or standing at the top of a black-diamond ski run. We can pray any place or time we're awake. (And as we will see, God has often spoken to his followers in dreams as well. Maybe the only time some of us are quiet enough to listen to God's part of the conversation is when we're asleep!)

BUT HOW DO I *HEAR* HIM?

Hearing from God during our conversations is one of the trickier aspects to grasp. You and I are physical, flesh-and-blood human beings. We use vocal cords and eardrums or hands and eyes to communicate with one another. Although some people claim to have extrasensory perception, for most human beings to receive our messages we usually need to compose our thoughts into words by speaking or writing them.

God, on the other hand, *can* read our minds and hear our thoughts. (Some people who are experienced at prayer say that we don't even have to form words in our minds to pray —

God can hear and respond to our feelings and emotions. What a wild concept! I admit I'm not there yet.) We don't need to speak our prayers out loud for God to hear them, although *we* may benefit from that.

Hearing God in return is even trickier because God rarely chooses to speak to us in an audible voice. If you tell some people you've heard God speaking to you, they'll try to get you locked up; yet when you listen to some people, they're constantly saying, "The Lord told me to . . ." What do we make of this difference of opinion?

The overwhelming teachings of the Bible are that God does answer prayer and that he's a full partner in our prayer-conversations. He does not, however, talk like you and I do. God responds through our prayers by using the Holy Spirit to convict us of sin and to move us to action; God answers prayer by speaking though the body of Christ, our fellow Christians; and God surely speaks to us through his holy Word, the Bible, his ultimate offering to the conversation.

PRAYER IN THE EARLY YEARS

Prayer is a part of every religion known to humankind. In one form or another, all people who believe in a supreme being desire to communicate with that being. Most religions teach that we're dependent upon a higher power. Out of that dependence, we make our needs known to our god — or gods.

Ancient civilizations such as Greece and Rome abounded with gods, most of which had human attributes and appetites. Conversations between deities and humans went like this: Humans communicated with their gods by offering sacrifices to appease the gods' tempestuous wrath (and consequently avoid storms, war, pestilence, illness, fire, and hardships of every sort) and to earn good fortune (and consequently receive proper weather, bountiful harvests, good health, plenty of wealth, victory in battle, and blessings of every other kind). The gods communicated to humans via augurs, Roman religious officials who read the future in the clouds, in the flights of birds, in animal entrails, and so forth. The augurs' announcements were known as auguries. This process doesn't seem like prayer to us, but that was how god-to-human communication was practiced at the time Jesus introduced the world to a much more intimate communication with God.

The Israelites didn't pray like everyone else in the ancient world, of course. The Old Testament records dozens of prayers by men and women, prophets and poets, kings and shepherds. In coming chapters, we'll see how the prayers of God's chosen people transpired over the centuries. As his people better understood God and their relationship to him, their prayer lives reflected those newfound understandings.

Then Jesus arrived, introducing a whole new type of relationship between God and his people. The first-century Christians built on the prayer foundation laid by their Hebrew ancestors. With this two thousand–year history, Christian prayer was substantially different from the other religions of the first century. Let's take a look at three key points about first-century Christian prayer.

THERE IS ONE GOD, NOT MANY.

Like the Jews before them, Christians prayed only to one God. Israel's neighbors believed that a male god and a female god created the world by conceiving and giving birth to the universe, including other gods. Instead of dividing their time to pray to two or more gods or trying to figure out which god might be most interested in their current predicaments, Christians were able to offer their prayers exclusively to one God, knowing that, as Lord of all creation, he was the God to pray to.

PRAY TO WHOM?

In Jesus' day, Palestine was under the rule of the Roman Empire. The period of the first century A.D. was known as the

Pax Romana (the Roman Peace). The empire was kept peaceful by two principles: force and cultural pluralism. As long as people prayed to the emperor once a year and paid their taxes, they could enjoy the benefits of the empire while continuing daily life as they preferred and worshiping any god they chose. During the 150 years of the Pax Romana, many strange cults, sects, and religions popped up. In this mix, Christianity seemed like just another insignificant cult. Few in Rome even took note—that is, until Christians refused to pray to the emperor. That's when the persecution of the first followers of Christ began.

HE CARES ABOUT YOU.

Christians understood God, as the Jews did, to be a personal Being who took interest in the prayers of his people. People who worshiped pagan gods believed they were callous toward humans. These people continually offered sacrifices to keep the gods happy so they wouldn't turn their wrath on humans. Roman gods were up to mischief with one another constantly, and when they took on human form, it was to mock, tease, and belittle humans. In contrast, Christians believed that the Lord was invested in the lives of his people. Old Testament writings told of Yahweh, a God so concerned with the fate of his chosen people that he sent his Son to become a human:

> *[Christ Jesus] had equal status with God but didn't think so much of himself that he had to cling to the advantages of that status no matter what. Not at all. When the time came, he set aside the privileges of deity and took on the status of a slave, became human! Having become human, he stayed human. It was an incredibly humbling process. He didn't claim special privileges. Instead, he lived a selfless, obedient life and then died a selfless, obedient death — and the worst kind of death at that: a crucifixion.*
> (Philippians 2:6-8)

SO, THAT'S THE DIFFERENCE.

You can see how different the God of the Christians is from the pagan gods. Jupiter, Juno, Neptune, Apollo, and even the emperor (who was human though he pretended he wasn't) were aloof from the human experience. The God of Christians actually walked in our sandals for thirty-three years. I, for one, find this extremely comforting. The fact is, I'd much rather pray to a God who is humble enough to leave his heavenly perch to experience the joys and trials I experience. I join the Christians who through the centuries have found God so approachable because he met us at our point of need.

THE GOD OF MARS HILL

Just a few years after Jesus' death and resurrection Paul was in Athens, the one-time capital of the Western world, and still a hotbed of religious and philosophical thought. "The city," Luke wrote, "was a junkyard of idols" (Acts 17:16). Paul walked the streets of Athens, talking with anyone who would listen, until he aroused enough interest to be asked to speak on Mars Hill, a hangout for philosophers.

> *It is plain to see that you Athenians take your reli-*
> *gions seriously. When I arrived here the other day, I*
> *was fascinated with all the shrines I came across.*
> *And then I found one inscribed,* TO THE GOD NOBODY
> KNOWS. *I'm here to introduce you to this God so you*
> *can worship intelligently, know who you're dealing*
> *with.* (Acts 17:22-23)

Paul goes on to contrast the one true God with the gods and idols the Athenians had been worshiping. God purposefully made the earth livable for humans, he argued, and God remains close at hand, interested in our daily affairs. This sets the Christian God apart from the Greek and Roman gods and confirms the uniqueness of the Lord: *He cares for us, which gives prayer its purpose.* We worship and pray to the One who created the universe—including each one of us. He has a special interest in our lives, and he desires that we stay in close contact with him.

God wants to hear our prayers—the profound nature of this concept can hardly be overstated. Never in the history of humankind has any other religion believed in a God so personally connected with his people. We can pray with great confidence because the true God, the living God, Yahweh, the Creator of the universe, hears our prayers.

CHAPTER TWO

HOW DOES PRAYER WORK?

I can make you one promise: we're not going to answer that question in the next few pages! Followers of God have struggled with this question for centuries because it's not entirely clear how prayer works. We wrestle with questions such as these:

- How does God hear millions of people praying all at once?
- Why do some prayers get answered immediately, others later, and others never at all?
- If God loves us, why doesn't he answer all our prayers?
- If God answers only the prayers that are within his will, why do we pray at all?

I'll give you a hint about what we know of the workings of prayer. By the end of this chapter we'll have to settle on at least one conclusion: Much of how prayer works is a mystery to us. It can't be explained. However, we can look for answers to some of our questions in the Bible and in the history of the church. If you're one of the Christians who has struggled with how prayer works, if you've asked these questions, you're not alone. I recently received this e-mail from Joel, a college student:

November 15, 2002
From: Joel
To: Tony Jones

Tony,

I have a question regarding prayer. It seems like when we pray for something good, and it turns out well, we thank God for answering our prayers. But when it doesn't turn out as we asked, it's just "part of God's plan" or something else equally vague. Four possible explanations can be discerned from this situation:

(a) God wasn't answering prayers in either case. He had a plan one way or the other, and that's what He did. If this is the case, what's the point of ever making prayers of supplication?

(b) God answered in neither case, and the results were totally of our world. Thus, prayer is also useless.

(c) God answered in one case and not in another. There wasn't a plan, implying a degree of randomness on God's part that I'm extremely uncomfortable with and think is unlikely.

(d) God didn't hear in both cases, implying that he is not, in fact, omniscient. This seems rather contradictory to our understanding of God.

How would you resolve this dilemma?

Joel

Joel didn't write this because he's unfaithful or because he's doubting his faith. He's just questioning the mixed messages he's received from the Bible, his parents, his church, and others regarding the effect of prayer. Let's face it — prayer *is* confusing. But it's also one of the greatest gifts God has given us, the opportunity to go to him whenever we want with our thoughts, concerns, pleas, joys, and thanksgivings.

I have a friend who was in the Marines during a time when the United States was poised for war. As the clock ticked down to the first moments of warfare, I knew Dan was only a kilometer or two from the battle lines. He would be one of the first soldiers in the conflict. What a comfort and relief to know that I didn't carry the burden of Dan's safety alone in my spirit. I could share my fear with God, knowing he's able to reach halfway around the world from me to protect my friend.

Still, some questions swirled around this comfort in my mind: *Would* God keep Dan safe? What does God think about war? Why doesn't God intervene miraculously into situations of conflict and bring peace? Prayer comes with unanswered questions.

WHO GOD IS

The trouble with understanding how prayer works ultimately stems from the character of God, our character as humans, and the relationship between the two. Let's start with God. As Christians, we believe that God is omniscient (all-knowing), omnipotent (all-powerful), and benevolent (all-loving).

God is omniscient.

Christians widely believe that God knows all things past, present, and future. In fact, many believe that God exists outside of time—meaning time is not a dimension that constrains him as it does human beings. God existed before he began the universe, which seems to be the start of time, so he must not be dependent on the clock. We also know that God cares about beings as small as pet canaries and knows every detail of our lives, "even numbering the hairs on your head!" (Matthew 10:29-30).

If God knows everything about us, even what choices we'll make in the future, why do we need to ask him for what we want or tell him about what we're thinking? He already knows what we need; he already knows what we're going to pray; and he already knows whether he's going to give us what we ask for!

God is omnipotent.
God is powerful enough to do anything. As Christians we believe not only that God created the cosmos but that he sustains its function constantly. The universe would cease to exist without him. Furthermore, he intercedes in the processes of the creation however he wants. He has the ability to stop an earthquake, cure someone of cancer, and derail a terrorist bombing.

Libraries hold many books written by theologians and philosophers about why God doesn't step in all the time, why he hasn't cured cancer, why he hasn't caused peace to reign, and why he hasn't put an end to natural disasters. Libraries also contain scads of books containing stories of God's miraculous intervention. One of my good friends and a volunteer with our church's youth ministry knows beyond the shadow of a doubt that God cured her of cancer ten years ago because of her friends' prayers. Now she runs a prayer ministry.

God is benevolent.

We know that God is good. He wants the best for us, and he's not out to harm us. In fact, the basis of Christianity is that God loves us enough to see his own Son sacrificed on our behalf. We pray to God knowing he's on our side.

When we combine God's benevolent characteristic with his omnipotence, we're nearly compelled to ask, "Why doesn't God just go ahead and make everything right without us having to ask?" Because God is all-loving and all-powerful, he could (and perhaps should?) cure all cancer, diabetes, and AIDS; stop every car accident before it happens; and bring peace to war-torn places with the snap of his fingers. Why doesn't he?

WHO WE ARE

Humans are *so* different from God. A brief look at our limitations will help us to see why prayer remains something of a mystery.

We have limited knowledge.

Unlike God, we don't see past, present, and future. We can't see around the world, much less see the entire universe in a single glance. We cannot see the big picture. We're limited in our ability to see and know, so we're often trying to understand God's eternal purposes in the context of our limited visibility.

Paul put it this way: "We don't yet see things clearly. We're squinting in a fog, peering through a mist" (1 Corinthians 13:12).

The result of our limited knowledge can be skepticism. We may doubt because we don't see the full story God is writing. We see only a chapter—or a page. What seems like a badly written story to us (which may cause us to doubt) makes perfect sense to the author.

We have limited power.

Although God can do *anything* he wants, we're not so unrestrained. As humans, we're bound by time, by three dimensions, and by our physical bodies. Even with advancements in technology, we're still mostly bound to this globe. We can fly around it at thirty-five thousand feet, a few of us can even get as far as the moon, but that's about it. And the skin that encases us imposes limitations on our abilities to make changes.

The human response to these limitations is to seek more power. The more power we attain—ultimately a quest to be like God—the more prideful we become. This issue was the downfall of Adam and Eve, and we've followed diligently in their footsteps ever since. This is the opposite of how we should be praying. We need humility—a spirit that recognizes the limitations of our power and relies on God's power for everything we need.

We're sinful.

Because we've followed Adam and Eve into sinfulness, we consistently make mistakes that show how glaringly different we are from God. Our sinfulness distances us even further from God's big picture. God, the Perfect One, has nothing clouding his vision, but we have petty insecurities, pride, and sinful desires that keep us from having the unblemished view that puts events into perspective.

THE CONTRAST

When contrasted with the characteristics of God, a look at our limitations makes it clear why we don't always understand prayer. We just don't measure up.

God	Humans
all-knowing	limited knowledge
all-powerful	limited power
all-loving	sinful

Our limitations impact our communication. For instance, my wife, Julie, and I are able to communicate well because we can understand each other. We each know where the other is coming from. While God knows a lot about me (he created me; he lived as a human for thirty-three years, so he understands my desires, joys, and pain), I don't understand where God's coming from a lot of the time. This is the essence of faith: We trust that God knows more than we do and that he has everything under control even when it may not seem like it.

As I said before, the question of why some prayers seem to be answered and others don't has plagued theologians for centuries. We know, though, that our free will as humans has a lot to do with it. We have the freedom to follow God—or not. If God answered every prayer immediately, he would be little more than a fast-food employee, serving up whatever we order. We also know that trials and temptations are a part of life. They help us remember to rely on God; otherwise we tend to go our own way.

Ultimately, the full truth about prayer is a mystery—and that's not a cop-out. Prayer *is* a mystery!

BIBLICAL PRINCIPLES ABOUT PRAYER

Most of the rest of this book explores examples of prayer in Scripture. Considering them is extremely helpful as we attempt to reconcile our limitations with God's desire for us to pray. Before we investigate them, let's look at three general principles about prayer in the Bible.

We can question God . . . to a point.

God made us with inquisitive minds. That's a good thing, but the problem with it is we aren't wired to simply accept the destiny, the plans that God has for us. The first response many of us have when something bad happens to us is to lament, *God, why did you allow this to happen?* Is it sinful to question God? According to the Bible, not necessarily.

In fact God himself is responsible for this. As we found in the last chapter, God created us to have relationships with him. This is what separates Christianity from all other religions. God didn't make our relationships with him one-way — he talks, we listen. He wants us to listen to him *and* talk with him. He wants to be in conversation with us.

Look at Moses, who on more than one occasion confronted God when God was about to wipe out the stubborn, hardheaded Israelites. Each time, God relented. God *changed his mind* in the face of Moses' pleas for mercy in Exodus 32:9-14, and because of Moses' reasoning in Numbers 14:10-23. These events raise all sorts of new questions: What does God know about the future? Did God know in advance he would change his mind? Is this event some sort of biblical literary device?

While theologians continue to debate these questions, this point is clear: When Moses took his concerns to God, even about God's plan for his people, God responded to Moses' prayers.

God's allowance for our questions isn't boundless, though. We still need to recognize our limitations as humans. We're reminded by Paul, "Who in the world do you think you are to second-guess God? Do you for one moment suppose any of us knows enough to call God into question?" (Romans 9:20). In the Old Testament, God's response to Job's questions is quite stern:

> *"Why do you confuse the issue?*
>> *Why do you talk without knowing what you're*
>> *talking about?*
> *Pull yourself together, Job!*
>> *Up on your feet! Stand tall!*
> *I have some questions for you,*
>> *and I want some straight answers.*
> *Where were you when I created the earth?*
>> *Tell me, since you know so much!*
> *Who decided on its size? Certainly you'll know that!*
>> *Who came up with the blueprints and measure-*
>> *ments?"* (Job 38:2-5)

God can handle our questions, but we need to remember who we're talking to!

God wants us to pray.

The second point to be made from Scripture is that God truly wants to hear from us. In a verse many people commit to memory, Paul wrote, "Don't fret or worry. Instead of worrying, pray. Let petitions and praises shape your worries into prayers, letting God know your concerns. Before you know it, a sense of God's wholeness, everything coming together for good, will come and settle you down" (Philippians 4:6-7).

This may seem like an obvious point, but we should find this truth quite extraordinary when we think about it. The God of the universe wants limited, finite, short-lived human beings to be in constant contact with him. How awesome! How humbling! What a great privilege! What a great responsibility!

Apparently, even though God knows everything we're going to ask, he wants us to ask anyway. Maybe this is for our own good, so we'll constantly remember to rely upon him. Maybe the process of making our requests known to God makes them real to us. Maybe talking with God helps us distinguish what we really need from what we only think we need. In any case, God clearly wants us to participate in the conversation.

Be persistent.

A biblical key to prayer is that we be persistent and direct in our conversation with God. Jesus makes this point:

"Here's what I'm saying:

Ask and you'll get;
Seek and you'll find;
Knock and the door will open.

Don't bargain with God. Be direct. Ask for what you
need. This is not a cat-and-mouse, hide-and-seek
game we're in. If your little boy asks for a serving of
fish, do you scare him with a live snake on his plate?
If your little girl asks for an egg, do you trick her
with a spider? As bad as you are, you wouldn't think
of such a thing —you're at least decent to your own
children. And don't you think the Father who con-
ceived you in love will give the Holy Spirit when you
ask him? (Luke 11:9-13)

Just before making these comments, Jesus told the story of a
man going to a friend's house for bread in the middle of the
night and bugging his friend for bread until he finally relents,
gets out of bed, and gives the man bread. In Luke 18, Jesus tells
a similar story about a widow bothering a judge to give her justice until he finally gives it to her. Jesus told these stories to
show us that we should "pray consistently and never quit"
(verse 1).

The admonition to persistence isn't a magic formula. Asking for our request repeatedly doesn't mean that God will necessarily grant it. Even Jesus, facing the Crucifixion, asked to be spared from it, but God proceeded as planned. Persistence should simply be a characteristic of our prayers.

WHERE WE'RE GOING FROM HERE

As our great guidebook for life, the Bible explains how to live in a healthy relationship with God, so we'll spend most of the rest of this book looking through the Bible from beginning to end to see how people prayed and what they prayed. We'll learn a lot from them, and we'll get a great gift: We'll be able to use their prayers ourselves.

Then we'll look at the prayers of godly, humble men and women who've lived during the last two thousand years. Many of them spent plenty of time communing with God, contemplating his nature, and considering other spiritual truths. They have insights that we can benefit from.

We'll be taking an awesome journey, tracing the prayers of God's people over four thousand years. Look for similarities and differences among them. Pay attention to the characteristics of the pray-ers and the prayed-to. Then add whatever you think of to enhance your own prayer time with the Lord.

Most of all, put this book down whenever you want to pray and *do it!*

PART TWO

PRAYERS FROM THE OLD TESTAMENT

CHAPTER THREE

PRAYING WITH
THE PATRIARCHS AND JUDGES

Conversation between God and human beings began in a way we can hardly even dream of. Adam and Eve spoke with God face to face! Sadly, their perfect relationship was quickly broken. After eating the forbidden fruit, Adam and Eve knew they were in trouble, so they hid from God among the trees. They did this when "they heard the sound of GOD strolling in the garden" (Genesis 3:8). Imagine that! God strolling in the garden. You hear him coming!

It makes you wonder—if Adam and Eve had the opportunity to stroll in the garden with God, why would they ever jeopardize that by eating fruit they were told not to eat? It seems like a no-brainer: eat the fruit and lose your incredible relationship with God, or don't eat it and be able to walk and talk with the Creator of the universe. Was the fruit *that* good? Was the serpent *that* persuasive?

We'll never know on this side of heaven. What we do know is the time Adam and Eve spent in the garden was incredible, if short-lived. After that, only Moses was fortunate enough to have such an intimate relationship with God: "And GOD spoke with Moses face-to-face, as neighbors speak to one another" (Exodus 33:11). Since then, we've all been on the same level, creatures looking to develop a relationship with our Creator through prayer.

Although tainted by Adam and Eve's misstep, at one time conversation between God and human beings was more like you and I think of conversation. We'll look at three characters from an early portion of the Bible—Abraham, Moses, and Deborah—and at a prayer by each of them.

ABRAHAM: DOUBT, THEN FAITH

Abram wasn't expecting God when God first called to him. We know hardly anything about him, except that he was married to Sarai and they were living in Haran. When Abram was seventy-five years old, out of the blue God told him to pull up stakes (literally!) and move his family to what we now know as the Promised Land, Canaan. Abram built an altar to the Lord there, but before long a famine decimated the land. Abram had no choice but to move his family to Egypt, where times were better.

He ran into some trouble there and was chased out of town by Pharaoh. Back in Canaan, this old man and his old wife once again pitched their tents. The old couple was child-less, an embarrassment in those days when a man's wealth was his family. Because they were both nearing one hundred years, they had no hope of that situation changing. Into their desperation God speaks:

> *After all these things, this word of GOD came to Abram in a vision: "Don't be afraid, Abram. I'm your shield. Your reward will be grand!"*
>
> *Abram said, "GOD, Master, what use are your gifts as long as I'm childless and Eliezer of Damascus is going to inherit everything?" Abram continued, "See, you've given me no children, and now a mere house servant is going to get it all."*
>
> *Then GOD's Message came: "Don't worry, he won't be your heir; a son from your body will be your heir."*
>
> *Then he took him outside and said, "Look at the sky. Count the stars. Can you do it? Count your descendants! You're going to have a big family, Abram!"*
>
> *And he believed! Believed GOD! God declared him "Set-Right-with-God."* (Genesis 15:1-6)

Here is an instance where prayer really is an actual conversation. Abram and the Lord have a dialogue about Abram's future. God's message to Abram is simple. It could apply to any of us: Don't worry; don't be afraid. I'm the God who created you, and I'll take care of you. When God first explains this, Abram's response is understandable. He doubts.

I wonder what would happen if I heard God speak this clearly. Would I doubt? Or would the fact that the Lord of the universe spoke my name confirm my faith 100 percent, for all time?

We know Abram's response was doubtful: *Sure, God. What good will your blessing be if you don't give me a child!?!*

How would you respond if God spoke to you in a seemingly desperate situation? Or think about it this way: How *do* you respond when God speaks to you in a seemingly desperate situation? God tells each one of us through the Bible and other means of revelation, "Don't be afraid; don't worry. I'm your shield." And how do we respond? Most often with doubt, just like Abram.

Abraham, as God began to call him later, is often referred to as the "Father of Our Faith," and for good reason. He had a normal, human relationship with God, a lot like you and I have. It was full of mistakes, wrong turns, times of faith, and times of doubt.

Let's also look at how God responds to Abram's doubt. God doesn't get mad at Abram. He doesn't lose his patience. Instead, he says, "Come outside and look at these stars. You're going to have more descendents than the stars in the sky. Count on it!" God doesn't see Abram's doubt as an insult or a challenge. God knows Abram's weakness as a human and that Abram can't see the future, so he reassures Abram that his future is indeed hopeful and full of children and grandchildren.

The result: Abram believes! It just takes a little patience and persuasion for God to convince Abram that he will, indeed, be blessed with an heir. This isn't the end of the story. When he doesn't yet have a child a few years later, Abram starts to doubt again. He has a son, Ishmael, with his wife's servant, Hagar, before Sarai finally gets pregnant and gives birth to Isaac. You can read about it in Genesis 16, 17, and 21.

What situation in your life do you have a hard time trusting God for? What will it take for God to convince you not to worry? How do you remind yourself that God is your shield? How can you follow Abram's example of being honest about your doubts, but ultimately relying on your faith?

MOSES: LOOKING TO GOD FOR LEADERSHIP

When you think of Moses, you might think of Moses the car-
toon character in *The Prince of Egypt*. When I think of him, I
think of Charlton Heston. That's the difference in our generations, I guess, but when I was in middle school (it wasn't *that*
long ago!), we had only four television channels. Every year
around Easter (and Passover, the Jewish holiday that coincides
with Easter), one of the networks would show *The Ten
Commandments*, starring Charlton Heston as Moses.

The movie takes almost three hours to trace Moses' life
from birth to death. *The Ten Commandments* defines the epic
genre of movies. That's also a good description of Moses'
life — epic. Saved from certain death as an infant, he spent his
first forty years as an Egyptian prince, watching his people, the
Israelites, being oppressed as slaves. After killing an Egyptian
to save an Israelite, Moses fled from Egypt and spent the next
forty years shepherding in the wilderness.

At the age of eighty, Moses returned to Egypt, this time to
free God's people from bondage. He led them through the Red
Sea and to the base of Mount Sinai. Moses climbed to the top
of the mountain to spend forty days with the Lord, receiving
all of the commandments and laws God wanted his people to
keep. When Moses descended from the heights, he found that

the Israelites had turned on God and created a golden calf to worship.

After taking care of the mess, Moses climbed back to the top of the mountain. He was discouraged and in despair, and he questioned the reason God had called him into leadership:

> Moses said to GOD, "Look, you tell me, 'Lead this people,' but you don't let me know whom you're going to send with me. You tell me, 'I know you well and you are special to me.' If I am so special to you, let me in on your plans. That way, I will continue being special to you. Don't forget, this is your people, your responsibility."
>
> GOD said, "My presence will go with you. I'll see the journey to the end."
>
> Moses said, "If your presence doesn't take the lead here, call this trip off right now. How else will it be known that you're with me in this, with me and your people? Are you traveling with us or not? How else will we know that we're special, I and your people, among all other people on this planet Earth?"
>
> GOD said to Moses: "All right. Just as you say; this also I will do, for I know you well and you are special to me. I know you by name." (Exodus 33:12-17)

We see some similarities to Abram here: Moses questions God's plan, and God has to reassure him a couple of times before Moses is satisfied. But rather than the issue being one of children, Moses is concerned about his leadership of this difficult group of people, the Israelites. Remember, ever since the burning bush when God first called him, Moses is a reluctant leader.

Once again, Moses doesn't know if he is up to the task of leading the Israelites into their unknown future. But instead of questioning his own strength, Moses makes it clear in his prayer that the people need God to be their ultimate leader.

Moses also essentially says to God, "I'll need to see your plans to know that you're on our side." And here's where it gets interesting. God *doesn't* comply with Moses' request; he doesn't open the future to Moses' human eyes. Instead he replies, "My presence will go with you. I'll see the journey to the end."

In response to that, Moses asks for God's presence to clearly take the lead on their trip through the wilderness, and again, God responds with words of ultimate comfort: "I know you well and you are special to me. I know you by name." And from that point on, God clearly does take the lead in the Israelites' forty-year sojourn in the wilderness. Despite some missteps by Moses and the Israelites, Moses and God have a friendship that lasts forever.

Have you asked God for something, but he hasn't given it? How did you respond? Where has God called you to be a leader? (Leaders aren't only up front and visible. Some people lead in service.) Have you, like Moses, prayed that God would be the true leader and your leadership would be empowered by him? What does it mean to you, as a leader in God's kingdom, that God knows you by name?

DEBORAH: AN ANCIENT SONG OF PRAISE

Some years after Moses led the people of Israel out of Egypt and after Joshua took them into the land that God had promised Abram, Israel was led by a series of judges. Moses picked the first judges, people who feared God and were known to be trustworthy and uncorrupt. on this side of heaven

After Joshua died, but before the people of Israel demanded a king, the Israelites attempted to settle in the Promised Land. It was a time of great turbulence. The judges, whose lives are recorded in the Old Testament book of Judges, ruled during this interim. They weren't quite kings, but instead were the heads of families who rose to prominence for their great wisdom. Gideon and Samson were two of the more famous judges.

Deborah, too, became a nationally renowned judge and prophet. She lived around 1250 B.C., and was known to sit under a palm tree (named after her!) to hear disputes needing her judgment.

One day, she summoned Barak, a general in the army. She told him God had spoken: Barak was to fight Sisera's mighty army. God had promised Barak the victory. Barak, not quite as confident as he should have been about this proclamation, was only willing to go into battle if Deborah would go with him. She agreed to go, but because of his cowardice, she announced, he wouldn't get credit for defeating Sisera.

As you might imagine, Barak's army crushed Sisera's army. Sisera fled from the battlefield and hid in the tent of a woman named Jael. After getting him sleepy with warm milk, Jael killed Sisera by . . . well, it was gruesome.

In one of the oldest Hebrew poems, Deborah responded to the victory God gave by singing a beautiful song of praise and thanksgiving. It takes up the entire fifth chapter of Judges. Here's a portion of it:

> *When they let down their hair in Israel,*
> *they let it blow wild in the wind.*
> *The people volunteered with abandon,*
> *bless GOD!*

Hear O kings! Listen O princes!
*   To GOD, yes to GOD, I'll sing,*
Make music to GOD,
*   to the God of Israel. . . .*

Warriors became fat and sloppy,
*   no fight left in them.*
Then you, Deborah, rose up;
*   you got up, a mother in Israel. . . .*
Lift your hearts high, O Israel,
with abandon, volunteering yourselves with the people—
*   bless GOD!*

You who ride on prize donkeys
*   comfortably mounted on blankets*
And you who walk down the roads,
*   ponder, attend!*
Gather at the town well
*   and listen to them sing,*
Chanting the tale of GOD's victories,
*   his victories accomplished in Israel.*

Then the people of GOD
*   went down to the city gates.*

Wake up, wake up, Deborah!
*   Wake up, wake up, sing a song!*

On your feet, Barak!
Take your prisoners, son of Abinoam! . . .

Most blessed of all women is Jael,
wife of Heber the Kenite,
most blessed of homemaking women.
He asked for water,
she brought milk;
In a handsome bowl,
she offered cream.
She grabbed a tent peg in her left hand,
with her right hand she seized a hammer.
She hammered Sisera, she smashed his head,
she drove a hole through his head.
He slumped at her feet. He fell. He sprawled.
He slumped at her feet. He fell.
Slumped. Fallen. Dead. . . .

Thus may all GOD's *enemies perish,*
while his lovers be like the unclouded sun.
(Judges 5:2-3,7,9-12,24-27,31)

Of course we agree with Deborah that when the Lord does a great thing for us, we should respond with a song of praise. But what's special about Deborah's song is that she is the only judge who responds this way. While over and over again in the book of Judges the people turned their backs on God, and then God still rescued them from certain defeat, only Deborah says, "Hold everything! We need to sing a hymn of praise to the God who has granted us victory!"

Abraham laughed with joy as a response to finally having a son, and Moses gave a long and beautiful speech to all the people before he died, reminding them to stay true to the Lord. But Deborah breaks into song, the way most of us do every Sunday in church, as a way of thanking God.

There's another interesting note about Deborah's song: In it, she tells everyone in the nation to sing praises to God. This is not her personal song; it's a national anthem of praise to God. She encourages all the people to stop what they're doing, to wake up, and to sing out to the Lord who has saved them.

When did you last wholeheartedly sing your praises to God? What was the reason for your praise? What's your favorite song of praise? Some of our national songs, such as **God Bless America** *and* **My Country 'Tis of Thee,** *are national songs of praise to God. The next time you sing one of these songs, sing it as a prayer.*

CHAPTER FOUR

PRAYING WITH THE PSALMISTS

Right in the center of the Bible, at its heart, is Psalms, the song-book of Scripture. You'll find 150 songs there. We don't have the original music that went with any of them, but they've been said and sung, a cappella and with instruments, for thousands of years.

Not only the Bible's songbook, Psalms is also the Bible's prayer book. All the psalms are written to God; every one is a prayer. All sorts of prayers are represented, written by several different hands. The types of psalms include songs of penitence, hymns of praise, prayers of thanksgiving, festival songs, and prayers of trust.

Book upon book has been written on praying with the psalms, so to look at just three of them is to only scratch the surface of what the book of Psalms has to offer. We'll look at a psalm from three distinct genres to give you a good start.

PSALM 136: A STORY-PRAYER

One unique aspect of Judaism and Christianity is that they are story-based religions. While other religions are based on beliefs about God and theories about how human beings can gain access to heaven, the Judeo-Christian tradition is inseparable from the stories of the Creation, of Abraham and Sarah, of Moses and the Exodus, of the kings and the prophets. And the Hebrew and Christian Scriptures, while they contain some laws and codes, are really focused on telling the story of God and his people. And, of course, Christianity has another unique aspect to add to this story: God sent his Son to be a human being and live among us. In becoming Jesus of Nazareth, God became a part of our story, the story of the human race.

The Bible is a record of this story, at least up until about A.D. 100. Since then, the story has been written by the Holy Spirit in the lives of Christians. In the Bible, the story is always important. The prophets constantly referred to previous events, reminding the people of what God had done for them. Jesus looked back when he explained that he had come to fulfill what the law and prophets started. The apostle Paul consistently reflected on the Hebrew Scriptures to show the importance of Christ in the overall work of God's kingdom.

The psalmists were no different. Five psalms can be classified as storytelling psalms—78, 105, 106, 135, and 136. In all of these prayers, the people of Israel were reminded of what God had done for them in the past, how he had been steadfastly faithful to them regardless of their lack of faith in him.

The psalms were often sung as corporate prayers, especially at times of celebration and festivals. As you read Psalm 136, imagine thousands of God's people gathered in the courtyard around Solomon's Temple in Jerusalem. High on the steps, a choir of priests sings out this prayer to God, and at the end of each stanza, all the people sing back in response, *"His love never quits!"*

Thank GOD! He deserves your thanks.
    His love never quits.
Thank the God of all gods,
    His love never quits.
Thank the Lord of all lords.
    His love never quits.

Thank the miracle-working God,
    His love never quits.
The God whose skill formed the cosmos,
    His love never quits.
The God who laid out earth on ocean foundations,
    His love never quits.
The God who filled the skies with light,
    His love never quits.
The sun to watch over the day,
    His love never quits.

Moon and stars as guardians of the night,
  His love never quits.
The God who struck down the Egyptian firstborn,
  His love never quits.
And rescued Israel from Egypt's oppression,
  His love never quits.
Took Israel in hand with his powerful hand,
  His love never quits.
Split the Red Sea right in half,
  His love never quits.
Led Israel right through the middle,
  His love never quits.
Dumped Pharaoh and his army in the sea,
  His love never quits.
The God who marched his people through the desert,
  His love never quits.
Smashed huge kingdoms right and left,
  His love never quits.
Struck down the famous kings,
  His love never quits.
Struck Sihon the Amorite king,
  His love never quits.
Struck Og the Bashanite king,
  His love never quits.
Then distributed their land as booty,
  His love never quits.

Handed the land over to Israel.
His love never quits.

God remembered us when we were down,
His love never quits.
Rescued us from the trampling boot,
His love never quits.
Takes care of everyone in time of need.
His love never quits.
Thank God, who did it all!
His love never quits!

Let's think about what this kind of storytelling prayer accomplishes.

It reminds us about God's character and actions. As the people sing it, whether at a great festival or in the privacy of their own homes, they are reminded about all God has done for them. He created the world, the air we breathe, the sun that sustains life, water to drink, and the soil that nourishes crops. Because God has done all this, surely he wants the best for us. The Lord rescued his people from the oppression of Egyptian slavery and brought them into the Promised Land. There he struck down king after king so his people could have the land he had given them. After he had done all that, why would he let them perish?

This psalm is also an encouragement, building confidence that God will continue to be good to his people. History has shown God is faithful and true, and because he's consistent he'll continue to be so. The story hasn't ended yet. God continues to move in our lives and continues to write his story.

This story-prayer teaches. The young ones who are hearing it for the first or second time are not only praying, they're also learning their history—our history—as they hear of great battles and heroism, of victory and triumph by God. You can imagine this song being sung as a bedtime lullaby three thousand years ago, or today.

The refrain makes the point over and over—twenty-six times—that God's love never fails. The Hebrew word for love in this psalm is *hesed*, which communicates the same concept as the New Testament word for grace. *Hesed* means steadfast love, love that has no conditions and no strings attached. It means love that will never quit.

Even as you prayed and read this psalm just moments ago, you probably got hooked on the cadence of repeating "His love never quits!" Think what it does to have that phrase bouncing around in your soul all day.

If you were to sing of your life with God, what kind of music would you set it to? What are the major events in your life that have shown you God's faithfulness? Pray those events to God. Create your own refrain about his love for you to incorporate into your song.

PSALM 93: AN ENTHRONEMENT SONG

We're not familiar with what it means to live under a king or to live like one. Even though kings and queens are the most common type of leadership humans have known, these days they're relatively rare. The ones that do exist usually have ceremonial and powerless roles. So we need some imagination when we find language in the Bible about God as king and about earthly kings.

A king is more than a president or a prime minister. He isn't voted into power; he gets his power from either his birthright or from taking it by force. And no matter how a king acquires his kingship, he has to use power over others to keep it. Therefore, a king is someone to be feared and respected. A king also deserves the thanks of his subjects because he's responsible for their peace and safety and maybe their food as well. A good king makes life grand, and a bad king makes life miserable.

With this in mind, let's turn to one of the kingly psalms. These psalms all preach the same good news: God is the King above all kings, and he is the ultimate good king. The Israelites held a festival every year in the fall to celebrate God's kingship over the universe and his triumph over all of Israel's enemies. God was enthroned, symbolically, during a ceremony. Among others, Psalm 93 was sung during this ceremony:

> *GOD is King, robed and ruling,*
> *GOD is robed and surging with strength.*
>
> *And yes, the world is firm, immovable,*
> *Your throne ever firm—you're Eternal!*
>
> *Sea storms are up, GOD,*
> *Sea storms wild and roaring,*
> *Sea storms with thunderous breakers.*
>
> *Stronger than wild sea storms,*
> *Mightier than sea-storm breakers,*
> *Mighty GOD rules from High Heaven.*
>
> *What you say goes—it always has.*
> *"Beauty" and "Holy" mark your palace rule,*
> *GOD, to the very end of time.*

Interestingly, this enthronement prayer isn't about God's power over earthly kings, but instead about his kingship over nature. Although we hear about an occasional oil freighter sinking or a ship running aground, we don't have much fear of the ocean. But three thousand years ago, sea storms were up there with earthquakes and volcanoes as some of the most fearsome natural events human beings could encounter.

With no Doppler radar or friendly TV meteorologist to warn of them, storms would come, seemingly out of nowhere, to imperil ships upon the sea. Boats were tossed to and fro at the storm's whim, with prayers to God as the sailors' only hope of escape.

In this context we see what a powerful message we send by singing that God is stronger and mightier than anything a sailor might encounter on the sea. Indeed, it reminds us of how astonished Jesus' disciples were when he calmed the storm on the Sea of Galilee.

This prayer refers to more than just the literal sea. Sea storms in Psalm 93 stand as a metaphor for chaos. The people who lived when this song was first sung were familiar with chaos. Most of what they experienced on a day-to-day basis was out of their control. Drought and famine could set in just as quickly as a rainstorm could flood them out. Diseases had no cures, and life was often short. Into this uncertain life came their faith in the God who created the world out of chaos, who is Lord over chaos, and who promises to never let chaos get the best of his people.

In some ways, our lives are far less chaotic today, but other, new forms of chaos and fear are part of our lives. We may know the weather a few days in advance, and we usually know where our next meal is coming from, but we are exposed to new uncertainties, new terrors that the Israelites knew nothing about. Considering metaphorical sea storms, Psalm 93 is just as applicable to us today as when it was first sung.

What are the chaotic elements in your life? What will help you remember that God is bigger and more powerful than the chaos? What does it mean for God to be your King? What does it mean for God to be King of the world? King of the universe?

PSALM 130: A LAMENT

Everyone has bad days, bad weeks, bad months, even bad years. Hard times are common to human existence. We all have things happen during the course of our lives that plunge us into despair—death of a loved one, a divorce, a lost job, a serious illness, an accident. You can make your own list, I'm sure.

You shouldn't be surprised, then, to learn that the largest group of psalms are the psalms of lament, songs for weeping, mourning, and generally sad times. Sixty-one of the psalms are songs of lament, sixteen of which are community laments, probably used during public fasts. The rest are individual laments, sung first by someone in great distress, and used by others in despair ever since, although maybe for completely different reasons.

Before one psalm of lament, Psalm 102, there is a single line of explanation that could be used for all of these prayers: "A prayer of one whose life is falling to pieces, and who lets God know just how bad it is." Psalm 130 is just such a cry for help. It's one of the Pilgrim Songs, a group of prayers sung by people who were making their way to Jerusalem for holidays. This song is a prayer of great beauty and power:

> *Help, GOD—the bottom has fallen out of my life!*
> *Master, hear my cry for help!*
> *Listen hard! Open your ears!*
> *Listen to my cries for mercy.*
>
> *If you, GOD, kept records on wrongdoings,*
> *who would stand a chance?*
> *As it turns out, forgiveness is your habit,*
> *and that's why you're worshiped.*

> *I pray to GOD—my life a prayer—*
> > *and wait for what he'll say and do.*
> *My life's on the line before God, my Lord,*
> > *waiting and watching till morning,*
> > *waiting and watching till morning.*

> *Oh Israel, wait and watch for GOD—*
> > *with GOD's arrival comes love,*
> > *with GOD's arrival comes generous redemption.*
> *No doubt about it—he'll redeem Israel,*
> > *buy back Israel from captivity to sin.*

All of the laments basically follow the same form: address to God, a complaint, a confession of trust in God, a petition for help, words of assurance, and a vow of praise.[1]

Psalm 130 has some unique elements for us to look at, too. The opening stanza is one of the most heartfelt cries for help ever written. The psalmist is almost begging in his prayer for God to listen, to pay attention, and to take action because "the bottom has fallen out of my life." Another translation states it this way: "Out of the depths I cry to you, O LORD" (verse 1, NIV). Every one of us can imagine praying this, calling on God to help us in our darkest hour.

A phrase in the third stanza also stands out: "my life a prayer." The point has come for the psalmist when the prayer and the pray-er have become one. They cannot be separated. He's like a watchman, waiting all night for the dawn, holding onto hope that God will indeed hear and respond. Here's the good news: God will come! What does a night watchman know? The sun always rises; the dawn comes without fail. Never has the morning not come. And never has God failed to respond to his people in distress.

Look back on your own life. Has God answered your cries for help? Has he responded? I'll bet he has. That's the message of all the psalms of lament, knowing that God will heed the cries of his followers. These are not prayers of despair or of giving up. In fact, if God *didn't* respond to our cries, we'd have no reason for lament. It wouldn't do any good. We cry out to God because God answers. We have faith that "with GOD's arrival comes love, with GOD's arrival comes generous redemption."

Have you prayed a lament to God? If your answer is yes, what was it about? Write a lament prayer that matches the structure of a biblical lament. Why does lamenting help us? Why is it comforting to see so many prayers of lament in Scripture? What have you experienced that gives you confidence that God is faithful, just like the dawn?

CHAPTER FIVE

PRAYING WITH THE
KINGS AND PROPHETS

The second half of the Old Testament is mainly taken up with two periods of history. The first is the era of the kings—Saul, David, and Solomon—who led Israel through the fairly brief period of unity and strength.

Around 1050 B.C., the people of Israel demanded a king from the Lord through his prophet, Samuel. Samuel objected, saying the people needed only God as their king, but the Israelites insisted. Saul was crowned king, and, although he was a great warrior, he ended up going mad with the thought that David was out to get him.

Although David was completely loyal to Saul, David did receive God's anointing and blessing while Saul was still ruling. David eventually became king, and he brought Israel into its heyday. At this high point, David's son Solomon ruled in what is called the Golden Age of Israel. Crops were bountiful, people were wealthy, and the great temple was complete.

After Solomon, Israel fell on hard times. The people turned away from the Lord and turned against each other. Civil war split the people into northern and southern kingdoms, each ruled by its own king. After about 150 years of turmoil, God began to speak to the people through prophets such as Isaiah, Amos, Micah, and Hosea. The prophets told the people to get back on track with God, they warned about the consequences of not doing so, and they pointed to the great Savior who was to come.

During this time, the old covenants, the ones that God had forged with Abraham, Moses, and David, were being neglected. The system of laws and regulations that kept the people in God's good graces wasn't working because the people weren't holding up their ends of the deal. Even when they were, the prophets cried out that their hearts weren't in it. The point isn't to keep the laws out of obligation, said the prophets, but out of love for the Lord.

This is our history, too.

Dozens of prayers can be found in these pages of the Bible — some of the prophets go on for chapters of unceasing prayer — but we'll look at just three: first from the wise king, Solomon, then from two prophets, Jeremiah and Daniel.

SOLOMON: A REQUEST FOR WISDOM

Near the beginning of Solomon's reign, he does what we hope any ruler would do. In 1 Kings 3, he asks God for wisdom. After Solomon marries his queen, he travels to Gibeon to worship at the shrine (before the temple in Jerusalem was finished). There, he and God have a dialogue. This one is different from the prayers we've looked at previously for two reasons: (1) the communication is initiated by God, and (2) it takes place in a dream. Neither of these differences disqualifies it from being a prayer. In fact, it falls perfectly within our definition of prayer being a conversation with God.

This isn't the first we hear about Solomon. In the previous chapter, we read that he was involved in the murder of three men and that he banished Abiathar the priest from the land. These may be the dirty but necessary parts of being king, but they're still a tough way for Solomon to begin his reign. It's with this in mind that the young king goes off to conference with God in Gibeon.

As the events of the story begin, we find a young man, overwhelmed by the fact that he now sits enthroned as king of Israel, sleeping.

> That night, there in Gibeon, GOD appeared to Solomon
> in a dream: God said, "What can I give you? Ask."

Solomon said, "You were extravagantly gener-
ous in love with David my father, and he lived faith-
fully in your presence, his relationships were just and
his heart right. And you have persisted in this great
and generous love by giving him—and this very
day!—a son to sit on his throne.

"And now here I am: GOD, my God, you have
made me, your servant, ruler of the kingdom in place
of David my father. I'm too young for this, a mere
child! I don't know the ropes, hardly know the 'ins'
and 'outs' of this job. And here I am, set down in the
middle of the people you've chosen, a great people—
far too many to ever count.

"Here's what I want: Give me a God-listening
heart so I can lead your people well, discerning the
difference between good and evil. For who on their
own is capable of leading your glorious people?"
God, the Master, was delighted with Solomon's
response. (verses 6-10)

Solomon doesn't launch directly into his request, not that it
would be unacceptable. Solomon first praises God for his
goodness to Solomon's father, David. The love God showed to
David obviously has left a deep impression on Solomon, and
the young king desires a similar relationship with the Lord.

Solomon even remarks on his own youth, and on the fact that God's love for David is so great that it extends beyond David's life. David is dead, but his heir is on the throne. Clearly, Solomon knows that his reign is dependent, not on his own strength or intelligence, but on the blessing of God. He is too young to be a good king, but with God's help he knows he might manage it.

Then Solomon gets to his request: "Give me a God-listening heart so I can lead your people well, discerning the difference between good and evil."

Think about what you would ask for if God were to ask you the same question. Would you ask for riches? Good health? True love? Solomon doesn't ask for any of these. He asks God for wisdom to rule over the Israelites, ultimately a selfless prayer. He put the people of Israel above himself, saying that their well-being is more important.

Solomon offers a prayer of great humility. He asks for God's wisdom because he knows his own wisdom is insufficient. Left on his own, Solomon would be no better than any other king, but invested with God's wisdom, he has the ability to rule with a justice that transcends human ability.

God is pleased with Solomon's request, and he grants it.

Soon after, we see Solomon's wisdom in action. Two women came to him, arguing over a baby. Solomon's decree was to cut the baby in half. One of the women shrieked in horror at the thought, which revealed her to Solomon as the baby's true mother.

Solomon's wisdom is further revealed in the biblical books of Song of Songs and Ecclesiastes (he authored both), and Proverbs (he wrote the bulk of it). Solomon went on to have a long reign, marked by superior wisdom.

Now, three thousand years later, Solomon is still known as the wisest—and one of the greatest—kings ever to rule. His legacy all goes back to a simple, humble prayer.

How can you remember to pray for wisdom the next time you're given a big task to accomplish or when you're put in leadership over others? Why is God's wisdom better than your own wisdom? Check your motives to be certain you aren't praying for wisdom as a way to get wealth, influence, or prestige.

JEREMIAH: RIGHTEOUS QUESTIONS

Four hundred years after Solomon, Israel was in a much different situation than it had been when Solomon was king. The

land was divided into two nations, and the kings were not
known for their wisdom or justice. Into this chaos, God called
twenty-year-old Jeremiah to be his prophet:

This is what GOD said:

"Before I shaped you in the womb,
  I knew all about you.
Before you saw the light of day,
  I had holy plans for you:
A prophet to the nations—
  that's what I had in mind for you."

But I said, "Hold it, Master GOD! Look at me.
  I don't know anything. I'm only a boy!"

GOD told me, "Don't say, 'I'm only a boy.'
  I'll tell you where to go and you'll go there.
I'll tell you what to say and you'll say it.
  Don't be afraid of a soul.
I'll be right there, looking after you."
  GOD's Decree.

GOD reached out, touched my mouth, and said,
  "Look! I've just put my words in your mouth—
  hand-delivered!

> *See what I've done? I've given you a job to do*
> > *among nations and governments —a red-letter day!*
> *Your job is to pull up and tear down,*
> > *take apart and demolish,*
> *And then start over,*
> > *building and planting."* (Jeremiah 1:4-10)

This boy, a young man really, didn't shirk God's call; he responded mightily. The book of Jeremiah is a record of his prophecies to kings and to the people of Israel. He spoke God's truth at a time of great social disruption, leading up to and including the fall of Jerusalem in 587 B.C. and the exile of the Israelites into Babylon.

Jeremiah's prayer comes from the early part of the book, where many of his prophecies are collected. Jeremiah is questioning God, even getting right in his face. In fact, this prayer is about one of the biggest questions facing human beings: Why do bad things happen to good people and good things happen to bad people? God promises in Psalm 1 that those who do good and follow him and his Word are like trees "replanted in Eden, bearing fresh fruit every month" (verse 3), while the wicked are "mere windblown dust— Without defense in court, unfit company for innocent people" (verses 4-5).

Jeremiah's experience, however, was the opposite. Evil people prosper. Good people suffered. The situation seemed unjust, so the prophet prayed to God,

> *You are right, O GOD, and you set things right.*
>> *I can't argue with that. But I do have some questions:*
> *Why do bad people have it so good?*
>> *Why do con artists make it big?*
> *You planted them and they put down roots.*
>> *They flourished and produced fruit.*
> *They talk as if they're old friends with you,*
>> *but they couldn't care less about you.*
> *Meanwhile, you know me inside and out.*
>> *You don't let me get by with a thing!*
> *Make them pay for the way they live,*
>> *pay with their lives, like sheep marked for slaughter.*
> *How long do we have to put up with this —*
>> *the country depressed, the farms in ruin —*
> *And all because of wickedness, these wicked lives?*
>> *Even animals and birds are dying off*
> *Because they'll have nothing to do with God*
>> *and think God has nothing to do with them.*
> (Jeremiah 12:1-4)

Which of us couldn't ask God the same questions? We, like Jeremiah, live in a world of confusion, chaos, and distress. We look around only to find many people who've become wealthy through their evil ways. Those of us who make godly, ethical choices don't seem to reap rewards. These observations directly contradict the promises of Psalm 1.

Even though we don't understand why good people suffer and bad people prosper, how many of us have Jeremiah's courage to challenge God? A prophet's main job is to confront the people with God's justice, but what does he do when *God* seems unjust? Is it okay to confront God? Should we quietly say, "Well, I guess God has his reasons," or can we say, "Hey, God! What's up? This is unfair!"?

The answer comes not only in Jeremiah's example, but also in a key point made in chapter 2: God wants to be in relationship with us, and prayer is our conversation with God. Are some subjects off limits between you and your friends? Well, maybe, but that's not the case with God. Everything's open. God isn't afraid of our questions.

If you read a little further in Jeremiah, you'll see that God's answer is of little consolation. "So, Jeremiah, if you're worn out in this footrace with men," God says, "what makes you think you can race against horses?" (verse 5). In other words, God is saying, "If you think it's tough now, just wait. It's going to get tougher." That probably isn't comforting to the prophet, but when you're in an honest conversation with God, you don't always get the response you want.

What are the big questions you've got for God right now? Ask him your questions. What answers does he give you? In your experience, is the world a just place where good and bad people get what they deserve? If not, does that trouble you? Ask God to help you understand him better.

DANIEL: A PRAYER OF CONFESSION

Scholars debate about when the prophet Daniel lived. He was either a contemporary of Jeremiah in the sixth century B.C. or he lived in the second century B.C., only 150 years before Jesus' birth. In either case, the context of Daniel's experience was similar to Jeremiah's: Israel was on the brink of total disintegration.

In the ninth chapter of the book of Daniel, the prophet is pondering Jeremiah's prophecies about the fall of Jerusalem. Jeremiah prophesied that Jerusalem's desolation would last for seventy years. This drove Daniel into a time of fasting and penitence, out of which came Daniel's contrite and eloquent prayer of confession:

*O Master, great and august God. You never waver
in your covenant commitment, never give up on those
who love you and do what you say. Yet we have
sinned in every way imaginable. We've done evil
things, rebelled, dodged and taken detours around
your clearly marked paths. We've turned a deaf ear
to your servants the prophets, who preached your
Word to our kings and leaders, our parents, and all
the people in the land. You have done everything
right, Master, but all we have to show for our lives is
guilt and shame, the whole lot of us — people of
Judah, citizens of Jerusalem, Israel at home and
Israel in exile in all the places we've been banished to
because of our betrayal of you. Oh yes, GOD, we've
been exposed in our shame, all of us — our kings,
leaders, parents — before the whole world. And
deservedly so, because of our sin.*

*Compassion is our only hope, the compassion of
you, the Master, our God, since in our rebellion
we've forfeited our rights. We paid no attention to
you when you told us how to live, the clear teaching
that came through your servants, the prophets. All of
us in Israel ignored what you said. We defied your
instructions and did what we pleased. And now
we're paying for it: The solemn curse written out*

plainly in the revelation to God's servant Moses is now doing its work among us, the wages of our sin against you. You did to us and our rulers what you said you would do: You brought this catastrophic disaster on us, the worst disaster on record — and in Jerusalem!

Just as written in God's revelation to Moses, the catastrophe was total. Nothing was held back. We kept at our sinning, never giving you a second thought, oblivious to your clear warning, and so you had no choice but to let the disaster loose on us in full force. You, our GOD, had a perfect right to do this since we persistently and defiantly ignored you.

Master, you are our God, for you delivered your people from the land of Egypt in a show of power — people are still talking about it! We confess that we have sinned, that we have lived bad lives. Following the lines of what you have always done in setting things right, setting people right, please stop being so angry with Jerusalem, your very own city, your holy mountain. We know it's our fault that this has happened, all because of our sins and our parents' sins, and now we're an embarrassment to everyone around us. We're a blot on the neighborhood. So listen, God, to this determined prayer of your servant.

> Have mercy on your ruined Sanctuary. Act out of
> who you are, not out of what we are.
>
> Turn your ears our way, God, and listen. Open
> your eyes and take a long look at our ruined city, this
> city named after you. We know that we don't deserve
> a hearing from you. Our appeal is to your compas-
> sion. This prayer is our last and only hope:
>
>> "Master, listen to us!
>> Master, forgive us!
>> Master, look at us and do something!
>> Master, don't put us off!
>> Your city and your people are named after you:
>> You have a stake in us!" (Daniel 9:4-19)

Confession is central to our faith. Like Daniel, when we com-
pare our own lives to the sovereignty, compassion, and justice
of God, we always come out feeling and looking sinful. We
just can't measure up to God—or even to the plans that God
has for us. We consistently fall short.

Whether it's as an individual or as a group of people, thor-
ough self-examination leads to confession. And, just as Daniel
prays, God's compassion is our only hope. We cannot hope to
crawl out of the hole we've dug in our sinfulness without God

lowering a ladder to us. Jesus, of course, is the ladder, but his life does not get us out of our obligation to be faithful in our confession to God. As it is with Daniel here, confession is a necessary part of our faith.

What do you have to confess to God? If you have trouble recognizing your shortcomings, ask God to show them to you. Use Daniel's prayer to help you confess your sins. What will remind you to pray Daniel's prayer or one like it regularly? Why is confession good for us?

PART THREE

PRAYERS FROM THE
NEW TESTAMENT

CHAPTER SIX

PRAYING WITH JESUS

From an early age, Jesus showed great interest in spending time in the temple in Jerusalem, his Father's house (see Luke 2:49). About two decades later, he was back in the temple, chasing out the money changers and saying, "My house is a house of prayer; You have turned it into a religious bazaar" (Luke 19:46).

As portrayed in the gospel accounts, Jesus' prayer life doesn't appear to have taken place in the temple or synagogues as often as it did in nature. Jesus made a habit of withdrawing to the hills, a lonely place, the wilderness, a high mountain, or the Garden of Gethsemane. He went off to pray before he chose his twelve disciples, after he heard of John's beheading, after feeding five thousand men (plus additional women and children), after healing a leper, before the Transfiguration, and finally to prepare for his journey to the cross.

Most of Jesus' prayers were private. He taught his disciples to pray privately to guard against pride in lofty speech or preaching to bystanders under the auspices of prayer. However, two of his prayers are recorded: the Lord's Prayer and what is sometimes known as his high priestly prayer, which takes up the entire seventeenth chapter of John.

Jesus' prayer in John 17 is a beautiful and intricate prayer that he prayed with his disciples on the night before his crucifixion. I encourage you to read it because Jesus not only prayed for his followers whom he was about to leave behind, but also for you and me, that all who would later believe in him might be united to one another: "The goal is for all of them to become one heart and mind" (verse 21). Through this prayer, we also get a glimpse of Jesus' prayer life with his Father.

Introducing us to pray to the Father is significant. Throughout the Gospels, Jesus referred to God as "my Father in heaven." This was natural because Jesus is the Son of God, but what was unusual and profound is that Jesus taught his disciples to address God as Father. When Jesus taught his disciples (and, by extension, us) to pray, he addressed God as *Abba*. Though you may see it translated as "our Father," the meaning is closer to "Poppa." *Abba* is an intimate term for Dad. It actually comes from baby talk. This was shocking during Jesus' day because Jews were forbidden from even speaking God's name, and there he was telling his disciples to call God "Poppa"! Jesus had this kind of relationship with God, and he wants us to be able to pray to God with the same intimacy.

We saw in chapter 2 that Jesus' teaching in Luke was for us to be earnest and persistent in our prayers, not giving up until God answers, just as the man who bugs his neighbor in the middle of the night for a loaf of bread. He also taught that our prayers should be prayed with faith and a forgiving spirit. After telling his followers that they should approach God with faith big enough to move a mountain, he said,

> *"That's why I urge you to pray for absolutely everything, ranging from small to large. Include everything as you embrace this God-life, and you'll get God's everything. And when you assume the posture of prayer, remember that it's not all asking. If you have anything against someone, forgive—only then will your heavenly Father be inclined to also wipe your slate clean of sins."*
> (Mark 11:24-25)

We can tell from Jesus' example that he followed his own advice. No matter how large the crowds surrounding him, he never became so self-important that he forgot to pray. Instead, whenever things were heating up or he was facing a big decision, he snuck away to a mountaintop or a garden and prayed about "absolutely everything."

THE LORD'S PRAYER: A PRAYER FOR ALL TIME

The Sermon on the Mount is three-chapters' worth of Jesus' teachings on a variety of subjects found in Matthew 5–7. Included in that address is Jesus' advice on prayer along with a model known as the Lord's Prayer. The teaching that precedes the Lord's Prayer is insightful. Jesus said,

> "And when you come before God, don't turn that into a theatrical production either. All these people making a regular show out of their prayers, hoping for stardom! Do you think God sits in a box seat?
>
> "Here's what I want you to do: Find a quiet, secluded place so you won't be tempted to role-play before God. Just be there as simply and honestly as you can manage. The focus will shift from you to God, and you will begin to sense his grace.
>
> "The world is full of so-called prayer warriors who are prayer-ignorant. They're full of formulas and programs and advice, peddling techniques for getting what you want from God. Don't fall for that nonsense. This is your Father you are dealing with,

and he knows better than you what you need."
(Matthew 6:5-8)

Jesus preached a message of simplicity and humility when it comes to prayer. He didn't give any elaborate formulas—in fact, he told us to avoid formulas and programs and pray from the heart. Jesus encouraged humility by directing us to pray in private and not make big shows when we pray.

Then Jesus taught those gathered around him how to pray. In Luke's gospel, the Lord's Prayer follows a request by one of Jesus' disciples: "Master, teach us to pray just as John [the Baptizer] taught his disciples" (Luke 11:1). In Matthew's account, Jesus launches into this prayer by saying,

"With a God like this [our Abba] loving you, you can pray very simply. Like this:

> *'Our Father in heaven,*
> *Reveal who you are.*
> *Set the world right;*
> *Do what's best—*
>   *as above, so below.*
> *Keep us alive with three square meals.*
> *Keep us forgiven with you and forgiving others.*

Keep us safe from ourselves and the Devil.
You're in charge!
You can do anything you want!
You're ablaze in beauty!
Yes. Yes. Yes.' " (Matthew 6:9-13)

We've already noted the importance of the salutation of God as Abba. Next come petitions for God to reveal himself, perfect his creation, and make our world on earth as wonderful as his kingdom is in heaven. All three are about God's overall relationship with his creation. They show our subservience to and dependence upon God, and they look to the end of time, when God will bring everything to perfect completion.

Although many of us skim over these petitions every Sunday when we recite the Lord's Prayer, this is a prayer of great power. To imagine that our homes, youth groups, or schools might become "on earth as it is in heaven" (verse 10, NIV) is a scary thing to ask for! For God's kingdom is a place of perfect justice and truth. At the end of time, all things will be set right, all injustices will be made right, all sins will be forgiven, and all illnesses will be healed.

We'd better take seriously a request for God's kingdom to come and for earth to be like heaven. In ways large and small, the world won't be the same when this petition is completely fulfilled.

Three more petitions follow: for God to provide our needs, for him to forgive us and give us the strength to forgive others, and for him to keep us safe from the Devil and the temptations he brings. "Give us today our daily bread" (verse 11, NIV) is how most of us know this first entreaty. In the original language, the meaning is closer to, "Give us today enough bread to get through tomorrow." Asking for bread is a metaphor meaning we're asking God to meet our physical needs. The prayer is asking for our physical needs to be met so we won't worry about having food to eat and can focus on the work of God's kingdom.

Forgiveness is so central to the message Jesus brought that it would be strange if Jesus didn't mention it in this prayer. Forgiveness isn't only about us asking for God's forgiveness, which we surely need; we also need help forgiving others. The world should know followers of Christ as forgiven *and* forgiving people.

Jesus tells us here to ask God for protection from the Devil and his snares, as well as from our own foibles. Few of us would deny our need for this prayer.

Some late manuscripts also add the doxology that many of us are familiar with: "For yours is the kingdom and the power and the glory forever. Amen." Although these words may have been added to the prayer later, the closing is an appropriate way to end such a simple yet profound prayer.

What we don't know for certain is whether Jesus meant for us to pray this specific prayer when we pray or whether he meant it as a model for our prayers. We do know early Christ-followers prayed this prayer frequently. By A.D. 60, churches were teaching that followers should pray the Lord's Prayer three times each day — morning, noon, and night.[1]

Because of its prominence in the Sermon on the Mount, and its importance to billions of Christians ever since, it continues to be the most familiar and popular prayer among followers of Jesus.

Do you think about the meaning of the words when you pray the Lord's Prayer? It can be a real challenge to stay mentally engaged when the words are so familiar. How can you keep mentally and spiritually connected when you pray the Lord's Prayer? How can you incorporate the Lord's Prayer into your daily prayer life? What do you learn from Jesus' teachings about prayer? Implement a change or two from what you learn to improve your prayer life.

FACING THE CROSS: A PRAYER FOR GOD'S GLORY

John's gospel takes a dramatic turn at the beginning of chapter 12. Everything up to that point has been about Jesus' three years of ministry across the Palestinian countryside. Chapter 12 begins with Jesus in Bethany, a suburb of Jerusalem, where Mary anoints his feet with expensive perfume. This event is the first step in the final week of Jesus' journey to the cross.

The next eight chapters describe the events of a single week between Palm Sunday and Easter, including Jesus' teachings during that week. Jesus was under significant stress as his crucifixion came near. He knew he would be executed to complete God's plan for the world.

We turn next to a prayer Jesus offers at the beginning of his final week on earth. Jesus entered Jerusalem on the Sunday before Passover to the crowd's shouts:

> *"Hosanna!"*
> *"Blessed is he who comes in God's name!"*
> *"Yes! The King of Israel!"* (John 12:13)

Several Greeks, in Jerusalem for the feast, approached Philip asking to speak with Jesus. When Philip and Andrew reported this to Jesus, he recognized the request as a sign the Crucifixion was just ahead. "Unless a grain of wheat is buried in the ground, dead to the world," Jesus told them, "it is never any more than a grain of wheat. But if it is buried, it sprouts and reproduces itself many times over" (verse 24). The thought of himself as the wheat is undoubtedly distressing, and out of that emotion, Jesus said,

> "Right now I am storm-tossed. And what am I going to say? 'Father, get me out of this'? No, this is why I came in the first place. I'll say, 'Father, put your glory on display.'"
>
> A voice came out of the sky: "I have glorified it, and I'll glorify it again." (verses 27-28)

It's safe to say any of us would want out of the horrifying experience Jesus is to encounter within days. Jesus admits he is feeling storm-tossed. The experience isn't easy for him. Even though Jesus of Nazareth was one with God, he was also human. His toe hurt when he stubbed it; he was sad when people rejected him; he felt tired at the end of the day; he was hungry when he hadn't eaten in a while. It should not surprise us, then, that Jesus was afraid of what lay before him. When we read the gospel accounts of the Crucifixion, he had every reason to be afraid. It was a nasty experience.

His words here echo his own teaching in the Lord's Prayer: *God's* will, not his own, be done. No matter the cost to Jesus, God should display his own glory. How many times do we put our interests on display even though our choice results in God's glory sitting in the backseat? How many times do we pray, "God, get me out of this!"? Many times! Of course, we're not going to be called upon to do what Jesus did, but we can still follow the example of Jesus' prayer for God's will to be done and for *God* to be glorified through our lives, even if it means paying a cost.

This is a prayer that can be frightening to pray. What if God answers it?! Who knows what God has in store for your life or mine if we surrender our selfish interests and let God's glory be our life goal?

Jesus receives a great confirmation to his prayer. A voice of thunder validates his choice: *I will be glorified in your choice.* God gives us the same affirmation—albeit without the thunder—when we pray for his plans and glory to take precedence over our own.

When have you felt storm-tossed? Did you pray that God would be glorified in your situation? If you did, what was the result? If you didn't, what was the result? How can you better follow Jesus' example in this prayer?

AT DEATH'S DOOR: A PRAYER OF FORGIVENESS

I can hardly imagine a person praying during his torture and execution. I find it even more difficult to imagine that person praying for his executors. But Jesus was no ordinary person. He loved people to the end, and he prayed that his Father would forgive the people who killed him.

What an extraordinary accomplishment!

I have a hard time forgiving my "enemies," and I've never experienced anything close to the agony of crucifixion. Maybe you have a hard time forgiving, too. But Jesus hung there on the cross—his life ebbing with every gasping breath, soldiers throwing dice for his clothes beneath him— and prayed,

> *"Father, forgive them; they don't know what they're doing."* (Luke 23:34)

The Bible records seven statements Jesus made on the cross (known as the "Seven Last Words of Christ from the Cross"). This is one of them. It has been lauded in stories, songs, and sermons ever since. It stands as a great challenge to us that we, too, would forgive those who persecute and execute us, whether they're after our bodies or our spirits. Forgiveness and reconciliation, as I've mentioned before, are at the heart of the message Jesus proclaimed.

We can assume that God did, indeed, forgive those responsible for Jesus' crucifixion. Sadly, the church wasn't so forgiving. For centuries, Christians persecuted Jews as the murderers of Christ. We are starting to undo that great sin, and we still hope to fully follow Christ's ultimate example of forgiveness.

Why is it so hard to forgive people? When was the last time you were forgiven? What did you do to need forgiveness? Who do you need to forgive? Are you ready to forgive that person? If your answer is yes, stop now to pray. If you're not ready, how about praying that God would help you get ready? Spend time thinking about how Jesus forgave you. (And remember, forgiveness doesn't mean the wrong wasn't wrong. Forgiveness means you give up your right to revenge.)

CHAPTER SEVEN

PRAYING WITH THE APOSTLES

When he was crucified, Jesus left his disciples confused and sad. They had thought that the whole Jesus Movement was starting to gain steam. Some of them high-tailed it to Galilee, while others sat together in an upper room in Jerusalem wondering what to do next.

When Jesus showed up again after the Resurrection, the disciples were thrilled *and* perplexed. What did this mean? Would he now take David's throne in the temple and rule the earth?

When he left again, swept up into the clouds to be reunited with his Father, they were dumbfounded. Was he ever coming back? How were they to carry on without him?

His first followers managed fairly well. From this band of a dozen, made up of the likes of former fishermen and tax collectors, grew a faith that now counts 1.8 billion adherents worldwide. They went from being *disciples* ("those who follow") to *apostles* ("those who are sent") when Jesus left them in charge. The directive he gave them to keep the movement going was simple:

> *"God authorized and commanded me to commission you: Go out and train everyone you meet, far and near, in this way of life, marking them by baptism in the threefold name: Father, Son, and Holy Spirit. Then instruct them in the practice of all I have commanded you. I'll be with you as you do this, day after day after day, right up to the end of the age."*
> (Matthew 28:18-20)

They weren't going about this task alone; the Holy Spirit would be with them:

> *As they met and ate meals together, [Jesus] told them that they were on no account to leave Jerusalem but "must wait for what the Father promised: the promise you heard from me. John baptized in water; you will be baptized in the Holy Spirit. And soon."*
>
> *When they were together for the last time they asked, "Master, are you going to restore the kingdom to Israel now? Is this the time?"*

He told them, "You don't get to know the time.
Timing is the Father's business. What you'll get is the
Holy Spirit. And when the Holy Spirit comes on
you, you will be able to be my witnesses in Jerusalem,
all over Judea and Samaria, even to the ends of the
world." (Acts 1:4-8)

The Holy Spirit arrived on Pentecost and gave birth to the church. The Holy Spirit empowered the apostles to travel throughout the known world, to preach the gospel, to make disciples, and to baptize many thousands.

That same Spirit enlivens the church today, giving us the power to preach, heal, and pray. Many Christians believe the Holy Spirit is a significant part of our prayers, both moving us to pray for what we need and delivering our prayers to God's throne. Some Christians believe that the gift of tongues Paul wrote about (in 1 Corinthians 12:30) is a special prayer language given to believers by the Spirit. No matter your theological positions, the Holy Spirit clearly plays a noteworthy role in the prayers of Christ's followers.

Now we'll look at three examples from the New Testament of prayers from the apostolic age, while people such as Peter, John, and James were leading the church in Jerusalem.

THE DISCIPLES: A PRAYER FOR GOD'S CHOICE

The first prayer we'll investigate is straightforward enough, but the action the apostles took seems curious to us. Shortly after Jesus "was taken up and disappeared in a cloud" (Acts 1:9, technically called the Ascension), and some time before Pentecost, Peter persuaded the other disciples to replace Judas Iscariot, to return their number to twelve. Peter quoted Psalm 109:8: "Give him a short life, and give his job to somebody else." He went on to explain that the replacement needed to have been a part of the Jesus Movement from the beginning at Jesus' baptism, through the years of Jesus' ministry, to Jesus' resurrection from the dead and his ascension. The criteria seemed to have narrowed the choices down to two: Joseph Barsabbas, also called Justus, and Matthias. The disciples all apparently agree with Peter on the criteria, because they prayed,

> *You, O God, know every one of us inside and out.*
> *Make plain which of these two men you choose to*
> *take the place in this ministry and leadership that*
> *Judas threw away in order to go his own way.* (Acts
> 1:24-25)

This prayer reflects their awareness of God's responses to Moses (which we considered in chapter 3): "All right. Just as you say; this also I will do, for I know you well and you are special to me. I know you by name" (Exodus 33:17) and the call of Jeremiah (see chapter 5): "Before I shaped you in the womb, I knew all about you. Before you saw the light of day, I had holy plans for you" (Jeremiah 1:5).

We see a common theme in Scripture: God knows us better than even we know ourselves. This is the reason we can pray with confidence for God's help, wisdom, guidance, and courage. God knows whether Justus or Matthias would make a better apostle because God sees inside these two men. He knows their thinking, motives, and character.

I'm not surprised that the apostles prayed for God's guidance to make such an important decision. In fact, it seems the natural thing to do.

What they did next, however, is a little disconcerting to most of us today. The apostles cast lots, which means they probably threw stones or sticks (*The Message* says they "drew straws") to find out which man God had chosen. While we might feel uncomfortable with the idea of throwing dice to discover God's will, this was a common practice in Jesus' day. Several big decisions in the Old Testament, including choosing Saul to be the first king of Israel (see 1 Samuel 10:16-26), were made by casting lots.

What we don't find is an explanation for how drawing lots works or how God worked through this practice. While it's accepted in the Bible, it never states that casting lots is a way for all God-followers in all times to determine God's will. So it's done rarely now.

Casting lots aside, the importance of this passage is how the apostles turn to God in prayer for their first big post-Jesus decision. Of course, just a few days earlier they would have been able to ask Jesus this question face to face, but without the possibility of a physical meeting, they instinctively go to God for guidance—and he doesn't disappoint them. He helps the Eleven to fill the vacancy with Matthias, who traditionally is believed to have brought the gospel to Ethiopia.

How does God knowing you "inside and out" affect how you pray? When was the last time you went to God for guidance before a big decision? What happened? Would you feel comfortable casting lots or drawing straws to determine God's will on an issue? Why or why not?

PETER AND JOHN: A PRAYER FOR COURAGE

A short time after Pentecost, Peter and John, probably with some other disciples tagging along, walked to the temple at

3:00 P.M. for prayers, as they did every day. A crippled man came and lay by the Beautiful Gate daily to beg for spare change and for prayers. (Crippled people were not allowed in the temple.)

On this particular day, when the man asked Peter and John for money, Peter said, "I don't have a nickel to my name, but what I do have, I give you: In the name of Jesus Christ of Nazareth, walk!" As Peter took him by the hand to help him up, the man's feet became firm and strong. He started walking and leaping and praising God.

Everyone who witnessed this miracle or its outcome was amazed—except the religious authorities. They were angry. Just after they thought they'd squelched the Galilean uprising by killing Jesus, Jesus' followers were performing a public miracle. The Holy Spirit had indeed come, as Jesus had promised, and now the apostles were able to perform miracles in Jesus' name.

This was Peter's first recorded miracle—the first by any of Jesus' followers—so he took a risk by telling the man to get up and walk. But Peter's faith was rewarded; the evidence was clear as this healed man raised a ruckus inside the temple. Emboldened by the miracle he had participated in, Peter began to preach with authority and volume to all who were gathered for afternoon prayers.

The authorities became more upset. Not only had Peter performed a miracle, he declared the miracle proof that Jesus had risen from the dead. He called on the people to put their faith in Christ. That was all the priests, Sadducees, and temple police needed to hear. They arrested Peter and John and threw them in jail for the night.

Peter's boldness grew even greater during a night behind bars. In the morning he challenged those who had him arrested. They realized they had no grounds to hold Peter and John, so they threatened the two apostles, warned them never to speak of Jesus again, and released them. Here's what happened next:

> *As soon as Peter and John were let go, they went to their friends and told them what the high priests and religious leaders had said. Hearing the report, they lifted their voices in a wonderful harmony in prayer: "Strong God, you made heaven and earth and sea and everything in them. By the Holy Spirit you spoke through the mouth of your servant and our father, David:*
>
> > *Why the big noise, nations?*
> > *Why the mean plots, peoples?*

Earth's leaders push for position,
Potentates meet for summit talks,
The God-deniers, the Messiah-defiers!

"For in fact they did meet — Herod and Pontius
Pilate with nations and peoples, even Israel itself! —
met in this very city to plot against your holy Son
Jesus, the One you made Messiah, to carry out the
plans you long ago set in motion.

"And now they're at it again! Take care of their
threats and give your servants fearless confidence in
preaching your Message, as you stretch out your
hand to us in healings and miracles and wonders
done in the name of your holy servant Jesus." (Acts
4:23-30)

As they were sitting in jail, Peter and John may have reminded
one another about Jesus' words from the Sermon on the Mount:

"You're blessed when your commitment to God pro-
vokes persecution. The persecution drives you even
deeper into God's kingdom.

"Not only that — count yourselves blessed
every time people put you down or throw you out or
speak lies about you to discredit me. What it means

> *is that the truth is too close for comfort and they are*
> *uncomfortable. You can be glad when that hap-*
> *pens—give a cheer, even!—for though they don't*
> *like it, I do! And all heaven applauds. And know that*
> *you are in good company. My prophets and wit-*
> *nesses have always gotten into this kind of trouble."*
> (Matthew 5:10-12)

Suddenly, Peter and John were a part of the long line of prophets and leaders who'd been thrown into jail on God's account. Instead of fearing persecution, they embraced it, because persecution was another sign that they were well within God's will. Jesus told them this would happen. They were no longer former fishermen on a quest; they were men of God, apostles of the kingdom.

Peter and John prayed in wonderful harmony that God would vanquish their foes. They didn't care about finishing off their enemies. They said in their prayer that they are leaving that up to God. Instead, they asked for more boldness and confidence to proclaim God's love, God's kingdom, God's reign in Jesus Christ.

This time, no voice came from heaven, but God gave a sign that he honors their prayer: the room they are in shook, and the Holy Spirit filled them with fearless confidence to go out and proclaim God's message. The result is a line from the Bible that we should all pray for our own time: "The whole congregation of believers was united as one—one heart, one mind!" (Acts 4:32).

Do you feel bold and confident to proclaim God's Word? If not, you've got a lot of company. Many of us don't feel bold or act confidently. How about praying for God's help to be bold—bold like the apostles—if necessary? Have you ever been persecuted for speaking about your faith? (In the Bible, persecution means jail, beatings, threats, loss of homes and property, exile, martyrdom.) If your answer is yes, how did you respond? If no, how do you imagine you would respond? What do you learn from Peter and John's example?

THE AUTHOR OF HEBREWS: A PRAYER OF BLESSING

We don't know who the author of Hebrews was, but the book comes from the era of the apostles and contains teachings that expand on the teachings of Paul and Peter. The book is actually a sermon, recorded for the edification of Christ-followers— specifically for second-generation Christ-followers who were sitting on their hands and dragging their feet (see Hebrews

12:12). They needed a theological kick in the pants to get them on track.

The preacher of Hebrews alternated between interpreting Scripture in light of Christ and encouraging the believers to re-ignite their faith. In Hebrews we see constant comparison between Old Testament personalities and Christ, who supersedes all they were and did. While the Old Testament dealt with earthly concerns, Christ in the New Testament is exalted, revealing heavenly truths to us. Because of him we can look back to the Old Testament and know that he is the fulfillment of the Old Testament prophecies and the perfection of its humanity.

Just as your priest, pastor, or minister probably does at the end of the service on Sunday, this preacher ends the homily with a prayer of benediction and blessing:

> *May God, who puts all things together,*
> *makes all things whole,*
> *Who made a lasting mark through the sacrifice of Jesus,*
> *the sacrifice of blood that sealed the eternal covenant,*
> *Who led Jesus, our Great Shepherd,*
> *up and alive from the dead,*
> *Now put you together, provide you*
> *with everything you need to please him,*

Make us into what gives him most pleasure,
by means of the sacrifice of Jesus, the Messiah.
All glory to Jesus forever and always!
Oh, yes, yes, yes. (Hebrews 13:20-21)

Benediction is Latin for "good (bene) speaking (diction)." In church, the benediction is the good word of blessing laid on the congregation by the pastor or priest at the end of the worship service. The Bible contains many excellent benedictions, the most famous in the book of Numbers. This benediction was given by God to Moses, who passed it on to his brother, Aaron the priest, to figuratively lay on the heads of the Israelites:

GOD bless you and keep you,
GOD smile on you and gift you,
GOD look you full in the face
and make you prosper. (Numbers 6:24-26)

In giving this blessing, the Lord said, "They will place my name on the People of Israel" (verse 27). A benediction serves the function of blessing the people with the name of God.

The author of Hebrews offers a benediction to bless the recipients of the letter-sermon. The first half sings praise to the greatness of God who created everything, brought order out of chaos, and ultimately sent Jesus to be our Shepherd. It's almost as if the first half of the benediction is meant to remind us that God is surely able to do anything we could imagine. If he's able to create the world and bring his Son back from the dead, then he'll be able to put us together, make us whole, and give us what we need.

Imagine becoming that which "gives him most pleasure." How many times we fall short of what God has for us! What a great blessing we receive from the preacher of Hebrews, who reminds us of truth: God remakes us by means of Jesus' sacrifice into something more wonderful than we already are.

Do you remember ever receiving a benediction of blessing? Do you believe that God can make you into something that gives him maximum pleasure? If you have a hard time believing that, you can talk with him about it— even challenge him to make such a fantastic transformation in your life. Write a benediction of your own.

CHAPTER EIGHT

PRAYING WITH PAUL

One apostle stands out from the rest: Paul. Although he didn't live or travel with Jesus during his ministry as the other apostles did, he's largely responsible for our understanding of the Christian faith.

First known by his Hebrew name, Saul described himself in Philippians 3:6 as "a meticulous observer of everything set down in God's law Book." He was steeped in training as a young person to become a Pharisee. He stood nearby at the stoning of Stephen, the first Christian martyr, congratulating the stone-throwers (see Acts 7:60).

The Lord had different plans for Saul's future. Jesus struck him blind as he traveled to Damascus, where he intended to persecute Christ-followers. This was the beginning of the most amazing 180-degree turnaround in human history. His influence continues all the way to our day.

First, Paul traveled with the gospel. While other apostles also took the Message to new areas, their impact was much closer to Jerusalem than Paul's. Paul made it his life's work to take the good news as far as he could. Your Bible probably has a map documenting Paul's missionary journeys. (Often the maps are in the back. Take a look!) The personal cost to Paul was significant, including beatings, imprisonments, and eventually execution. The worldwide spread of the gospel began with Paul's four missionary journeys.

Second, he took the Message to non-Jews, a group that ultimately includes me and possibly you. The apostles in Jerusalem were all Jews—as Paul was—and they were convinced that people had to become Jewish before they could become initiated Christ-followers, and more specifically, men had to be circumcised before being baptized. Paul argued against this position, stating that people could skip Judaism and become Christ-followers directly (see Acts 15). Paul even used one of his assistants, Titus, to prove that uncircumcised men can be full-fledged Christ-followers.

Third, Paul was responsible for writing over half of the New Testament. His letters to the churches he had planted give us great insight into the first churches, their challenges, and their successes. He also explained with unparalleled clarity who Jesus was and what he did. Jesus often taught in parables, explaining the kingdom of God in a cryptic fashion; Paul opened the doors to Christ-centered theology. His letters stand as the first and, in many ways, the greatest Christian theology ever written.

Nevertheless, Paul wasn't so much a theologian as he was a pastor. Though he felt called to plant churches (which by definition includes eventually moving on), his letters betray that he left a piece of his heart with every church he founded. When he heard that a church was struggling or was disappointed he hadn't returned, he felt immensely grieved, so he poured out his heart in his letters. He had a particularly tempestuous relationship with the church in Corinth. In 2 Corinthians, he referred to a painful visit and a letter with "more tears than ink on the parchment. But I didn't write it to cause pain; I wrote it so you would know how much I care—oh, more than care—*love* you!" (2:4).

The love of a pastor for his people is often revealed in Paul's letters—most of the prayers in his letters are birthed out of his love. He told a number of churches that he was constantly praying for them, and many letters even contain these prayers.

Clearly, Paul was a man of prayer from his first experience with Christ to the end of his life.

PAUL'S LIFELONG PRAYER: ON THE DAMASCUS ROAD

Paul's pivotal life experience is referred to as the Calling of Paul or the Damascus Road Experience—the day Jesus confronted Paul. Luke records the original incident in Acts 9:

> *"Saul, Saul, why are you out to get me?"*
>
> *[Paul] said, "Who are you, Master?" (His response is understandable for a man who'd been blinded by a bright light.)*
>
> *"I am Jesus, the One you're hunting down."*
> (verses 4-5)

Paul's retelling of the Damascus Road Experience appears in Acts 22. At that time, Paul had just been at the center of a riot in the Temple, people were out to kill him, and as he was being half-arrested, half-pulled out to save his life, Paul turned around to address the crowd. He gave an address (we would call it a testimony), telling the people how he was converted from being a persecutor of Christians to one of its foremost spokespersons. After telling about Jesus revealing himself on the Damascus Road, Paul explains what he does next:

> *Then I said, "What do I do now, Master?"*
> (Acts 22:10)

What do I do now, Master? A simple, one-line prayer. The first question Paul asks after the Lord gets his attention. *What do you have next for me?*

The question becomes Paul's lifelong prayer. He follows God's call to the ends of the earth, proclaiming the Message as people try to imprison or kill him, but he continually asks, *What do I do now, Master?*

In this simple response to a changed life, Paul sets an example for each of us who endeavor to follow Christ. His prayer is one we can pray every morning when we get up. His prayer is one we can pray as the clock strikes midnight on New Year's Eve. His prayer is one we can pray after walking across the stage to receive a high school diploma.

What do I do now, Master? is a question each Christ-follower should ask after the Lord brings us through a Damascus Road experience, or any time he brings us through one chapter of our lives and into another. We all have watersheds in our lives, major transitions from one thing to another. *What do I do now, Master?* is a prayer to be prayed on your way in or out of just such a time. It's a prayer you might need to pray right now.

When did you last ask God to lead you to the next step in your life? Did you follow? What's scary about asking God the what-next question? How might you incorporate Paul's prayer into your life?

PAUL PRAYS FOR HIS FRIENDS:
STRENGTH FOR THE COLOSSIANS

The book of Colossians is one of Paul's final letters, probably written toward the end of his life. Colosse was a medium-sized city in Asia Minor. The church there may have been founded by Epaphras, an associate of Paul. Paul wrote the letter to correct questionable teaching in the Colossian church. Before he gets to the heart of his letter, he offers an eloquent prayer:

> *Be assured that from the first day we heard of you, we haven't stopped praying for you, asking God to give you wise minds and spirits attuned to his will, and so acquire a thorough understanding of the ways in which God works. We pray that you'll live well for the Master, making him proud of you as you work hard in his orchard. As you learn more and more how God works, you will learn how to do your work. We pray that you'll have the strength to stick it out over the long haul—not the grim strength of gritting your teeth but the glory-strength God gives. It is strength that endures the unendurable and spills over into joy, thanking the Father who makes us strong enough to take part in everything bright and beautiful that he has for us.* (Colossians 1:9-12)

Paul pays the Colossians a great compliment, telling them that he and his coworker, Timothy, have been praying for them ever since he heard a church was born in Colosse. The essence of his prayer is for God to make them strong enough to do the work of the kingdom.

Paul knew a lot about this strength. It transcends mere determination to move the Christ-follower from endurance to joy. Paul had experienced the kind of joy that comes from staying true to the gospel and not wavering in the face of trials. His personal experience makes his prayer for the Colossian church authentic. He knows what he's talking about!

Finally, he reminds the Christ-followers at Colosse that God has bright and beautiful plans for them. He's about to launch into some arguments against the false teaching they've been subjected to. Some of his comments may be difficult for them to hear. But before he gets into these messy matters, he reminds his brothers and sisters in the Lord that on the other side of confusing conflict is a wonderful plan for them.

Who do you know who might need a prayer like this? Who would benefit from a prayer for endurance? A prayer to be discerning about false teachers? A prayer to see God's bright and beautiful personal plan? Pray for them now or set aside a small block of time in the near future.

PAUL PRAYS THROUGH PAIN: STRIFE WITH THE CORINTHIANS

Paul's relationship with the Corinthian church is legendary. He founded the church, along with Timothy and Silas, during his first visit to the city in A.D. 50 or 51. The church grew quickly as many people converted to the new movement. However, along with growth came bitter factions, primarily a split between poor and wealthy believers. The new believers also needed help with their questions about sexual sin, spiritual gifts, and false teachings on the Resurrection.

The books we know as 1 and 2 Corinthians are actually the second and fourth letters in Paul's correspondence with the church. Paul was in Ephesus around A.D. 54 when he wrote 1 Corinthians. He sent the letter with Timothy, hoping his admonition would stop the Corinthians from fighting for status within the church.

Second Corinthians, however, comes at a much different point in the relationship between pastor and church. After Paul wrote 1 Corinthians, he had shared a painful visit and a tearful letter with the believers in Corinth. In 2 Corinthians,

Paul wrote to explain why he hadn't come back to repair the relationships damaged by the painful visit. His letter is a long treatise on the meaning and value of ministry and its number-one concern: reconciliation.

With this in mind, we can see why Paul's prayer for the Corinthians takes on a much different tone than his prayer for the Colossians. It's a prayer born out of pain and anguish. He hadn't met the Colossians he had written to, but he knew the Corinthians—and some of them had hurt him with their words and doubts. This is the prayer at the beginning of his letter:

> *All praise to the God and Father of our Master, Jesus the Messiah! Father of all mercy! God of all healing counsel! He comes alongside us when we go through hard times, and before you know it, he brings us alongside someone else who is going through hard times so that we can be there for that person just as God was there for us. We have plenty of hard times that come from following the Messiah, but no more so than the good times of his healing comfort—we get a full measure of that, too.* (2 Corinthians 1:3-5)

Even in anguish and doubt, Paul finds reason to hope: God takes our painful times and uses them for good. After we experience hard times, we are able to help others going through difficul-ties. How many times has this proved true in your life? Just when you were wondering why God allowed you to suffer through a painful or lonely time, you have the opportunity to help someone in need.

Healing is a key point of this prayer, too. Paul needs heal-ing in his relationship with the church he dearly loves, and his prayer is that God's healing comfort bridges the breach that has developed. So, another thing churches might learn from Paul's prayer is to ask God for healing counsel in difficult times and through painful relationships. Too many churches have split into angry factions for a period of years, or worse, have completely broken apart. Paul's prayer for the Corinthians is a strong reminder that, though we experience hard times when we follow Christ, the good times always outweigh them.

Do you need to pray for a full measure of God's healing comfort? Do you have a relationship that needs healing and reconciliation? What does Paul's prayer teach you about the need to pray for healing? How can Paul be so sure that healing will come to his relationship with the Corinthians? How do you think this prayer was received by the Christians at Corinth?

PART FOUR

PRAYERS OF THE CHURCH

CHAPTER NINE

PRAYING WITH
THE ANCIENT CHURCH

Beautiful and profound prayers did not cease when the Bible was fully written. Library shelves are taken up with collections of the wonderful prayers that Christ-followers have written in the last two thousand years. Prayers cover every conceivable facet of life. Worship books on my bookshelves contain prayers to be used at the times of birth and death, marriage and military service, baptism and confirmation, graduation and ordination. They offer prayers for teachers, social workers, and elected officials, even for the consecration of new church buildings and homes.

Christ-followers have sought God in prayer since the first days of the church until today. Prayer is the heartbeat of the church, so we're fortunate that some of the best prayers in church history have been preserved in writing.

To choose just nine of these prayers has been a difficult task. I can't claim to have chosen the best—that's a subjective task. Ultimately, my choices reflect prayers that are important to me. I encourage you to search the library and the Internet for your own favorites and add them to your personal prayer book.

CLEMENT OF ROME: A PRAYER FOR THE NEEDY

Clement of Rome is one of the earliest church fathers we have information about. He seems to have known Peter and Paul, both of whom were martyred in Rome around A.D. 65. Peter may have personally appointed Clement to be the head of the church in Rome.

Clement wrote two letters, aptly named 1 Clement and 2 Clement. In the year A.D. 96 or so, he wrote the first letter to the still-divided church in Corinth, which was being read as Scripture in Corinth as late as A.D. 170. Second Clement is a sermon-letter about the characteristics of the Christian life, also written in A.D. 96, the year Clement died.

Clement offered a prayer in his second letter that's a wonderful example of how early Christ-followers were more concerned for others than themselves. Even at a time of horrible persecution—Clement lived during the first persecutions of Christians in Rome—Clement composed a prayer for those in need of God's good gifts. In Clement's day, Rome was much like a big city today, teeming with people in distress—homeless, hungry, imprisoned. As the head bishop in this metropolis, he prays,

> *We beg you, Lord, to help and defend us. Deliver the oppressed, pity the insignificant, raise the fallen,*

*show yourself to the needy, heal the sick, bring
back those of your people who have gone astray,
feed the hungry, lift up the weak, take off the prisoners' chains. May every nation come to know that
you alone are God, that Jesus Christ is your
Child, that we are your people, the sheep that you
pasture.* [1]

One of the reasons I love Clement's prayer so much is that it
was the inspiration for another prayer. The Book of Common
Prayer is the handbook for worship in the Episcopal Church,
and it contains orders of service for daily morning, noon, and
evening prayers. One of the last prayers of the evening service
is one I say nearly every night before I go to sleep. It reminds
me that no matter how badly my day has gone, someone has
had a worse day. Someone is struggling for life in a hospital
bed. Someone is sleeping under a bridge. Someone is fighting
depression so severe she doesn't know whether she wants to
live another day. Someone grieves the death of a loved one.
Instead of focusing on selfish or trivial desires, at the end of the
day I pray this prayer to remind myself that my faith needs to
be others-centered:

*Keep watch, dear Lord, with those who work, or
watch, or weep this night, and give your angels*

> *charge over those who sleep. Tend the sick, Lord*
> *Christ; give rest to the weary, bless the dying, soothe*
> *the suffering, pity the afflicted, shield the joyous; and*
> *all for your love's sake. Amen.*[2]

I love the fact that Christ-followers have been praying a form of this prayer since about seventy years after Jesus' resurrection. My evening prayer ties me to Clement and to millions of Christians who have lived between us. It links me with the great cloud of witnesses, the pioneers who blazed the way in faith before me (see Hebrews 12:1).

Are you sufficiently concerned for the world's needy? Does your prayer life reflect concern for them? How can you be more committed to praying for the needs of others, even people you don't know? Do you have a regular prayer that you start or end the day with?

ORIGEN: A PRAYER FOR INNER CLEANSING

Origen lived from about A.D. 185 until about 254, a long life for that time. He was a prolific author and speaker, writing hundreds of books and delivering hundreds of sermons. Much of what he wrote has been lost to us today, but we know that he caused controversy.

The third century was a time when biblical scholars and theologians were trying to figure out the relationship between Christ and God. Was Christ equal to the Father? Was his position beneath the Father, just like an earthly son is subject to his father? Origen's theories on the Trinity were a little too nebulous for some in the early church, for he seemed to place the Father, Son, and Holy Spirit in a top-down hierarchy rather than as coequals. Origen's answers to these controversial theological questions didn't interfere with his awesome faith. He was known to keep a strict life of fasting, poverty, and prayer. Here's one of his prayers:

> O Jesus, my feet are dirty. Come even as a slave to me, pour water into your bowl, come and wash my feet. In asking such a thing I know I am overbold but I dread what was threatened when you said to me "If I do not wash your feet then I have no fellowship with you." Wash my feet then, because I long for your companionship. And yet, what am I asking? It was well for Peter to ask you to wash his feet, for him that was all that was needed for him to be clean in every part. With me it is different, though you wash me now I stand in need of that other washing, the cleansing you promised when you said, "there is a baptism you will be baptized with."[3]

Origen has placed himself within the story of Jesus washing the disciples' feet. He imagines that he is attending the Last Supper, too. The Lord is ready to wash his feet. Origen recognizes Jesus' foot-washing as a metaphor for a deeper, spiritual cleansing that Jesus offers. You can almost feel Origen's heartbeat: he intensely desires God to cleanse him of his sin and make him right with God.

This is a powerful prayer. Origen uses Scripture as a guide and makes it intimate and immediate. He also makes clear the ultimate cleansing that is available only in the rite of baptism, which Jesus invited his followers into in Mark 10:39: "you *will* . . . be baptized in my baptism." Every Christian needs to be reminded of her or his baptism on a regular basis, especially when feeling trapped in sin.

So Origen's is a good prayer to have on hand when you're feeling like you've fallen short. The good thing is we know how to address the problem. When we ask Jesus to wash us, he always does.

Do you feel like your feet are dirty? Imagine yourself in the gospel story having your feet washed by Jesus. What would that experience make you think? Do you ever reflect back on your baptism (whether or not you can remember it)? If you haven't been baptized, is that some-

thing you're ready to do? What does your baptism mean to you?

JOHN CHRYSOSTOM: PRAYERS FOR THE WORLD

As a young man, John felt called to the monastic life, but his gift for preaching kept him from the seclusion common to many monks. He became the bishop of Constantinople in A.D. 389. By then he had already earned the moniker *Chrysostom*, which means "golden mouthed." He wrote and preached a great deal, much of it copied and handed down through the ages.

Sadly, after Chrysostom became patriarch of Constantinople, his attempted reforms of the city met with resistance by the Empress Eudoxia, who liked her sinful lifestyle and didn't want any churchman to rebuke her. She had Chrysostom banished, first to Antioch and the on this side of heavenn to the barren outpost of Pontus, on the edge of the Black Sea. As his health was failing, he was forced to march in severe weather until he finally died in A.D. 407 at the age of sixty.

The *Divine Liturgy of St. John Chrysostom* is the order of worship used in the Eastern Orthodox Church. While the liturgy has gone through many changes over the centuries (you'll notice distinctly modern references in the prayer that follows), it still embodies the great faith of its original author. The Great Litany is the prayer that leads ultimately to the Lord's Supper. Like Psalm 136 (see chapter 4), the Great Litany is a call-and-response prayer. The priest or minister sings out or says a prayer, and the congregation responds with, "Lord, have mercy." It's a prayer whose focus begins with the Trinity, encompasses many aspects of earthly living, and concludes by returning to the Trinity:

> *Blessed is the kingdom of the Father, and of the Son, and of the Holy Spirit, now and ever, and unto ages of ages. Amen.*
>
> *In peace let us pray to the Lord.* LORD, HAVE MERCY.
>
> *For the peace from above and for the salvation of our souls, let us pray to the Lord.* LORD, HAVE MERCY.
>
> *For the peace of the whole world, for the good estate of the holy churches of God, and for the union of all people, let us pray to the Lord.* LORD, HAVE MERCY.
>
> *For this holy house, and for those who with faith, reverence, and fear of God enter therein, let us pray to the Lord.* LORD, HAVE MERCY.
>
> *For the President, for all civil authorities, and for the armed forces, let us pray to the Lord.* LORD, HAVE MERCY.

For this city, for every city and country, and for those who in faith dwell therein, let us pray to the Lord. LORD, HAVE MERCY.

For favorable weather, for abundance of the fruits of the earth, and for peaceful times, let us pray to the Lord. LORD, HAVE MERCY.

For travelers by land, by sea, and by air, for the sick and the suffering, for captives, and for their salvation, let us pray to the Lord. LORD, HAVE MERCY.

For our deliverance from all tribulation, wrath, danger, and necessity, let us pray to the Lord. LORD, HAVE MERCY.

Help us, save us, have mercy on us, and keep us, O God, by your grace. LORD, HAVE MERCY.

Let us commend ourselves and each other and all our life unto Christ our God. To you, O Lord.

O Lord our God, your power is incomparable. Your glory is incomprehensible. Your mercy is infinite. Your love of humankind is inexpressible. Look down upon us and upon this holy house with pity, O Master, and grant us and those who pray with us your rich mercies and compassion.

For to you belong all glory, honor and worship, to
the Father, and to the Son, and to the Holy Spirit,
now and ever, and unto ages of ages. Amen.[4]

Though the Great Litany is meant for public worship, many use it for personal devotion as well. The constant refrain of "Lord, have mercy" reminds us that our physical needs, our safety, what little peace exists in the world, all we have, is a result of God's mercy. The litany also helps us focus prayer on people and topics we might not normally think of: government officials, travelers, and bountiful harvest.

Chrysostom's prayer ends with one of the most beautiful hymns to God ever composed. We sense how language is stretched to its limits to verbalize how awesome and majestic God is. Words such as *incomprehensible, infinite,* and *inexpressible* come close but are still lacking. God's nature and infinite qualities are ultimately beyond our ability to express through words. It's still important to try! God deserves our praise.

How might you incorporate Chrysostom's litany into your prayers? Make a list of people and concerns you might want to include more regularly in your prayers. Why not try writing your own prayer litany?

CHAPTER TEN

PRAYING WITH
THE MEDIEVAL CHURCH

The Middle Ages extended from the fall of the Roman Empire until the rise of the Renaissance. Some scholars date that period from A.D. 476 until 1453. Life in the Middle Ages has been described as nasty, dull, and brutish. Life expectancy was short. Outbreaks of bubonic plague, also called Black Death, took the lives of nearly one-third of the European people.

For Christianity, the Middle Ages were the best of times and the worst of times. Christianity flourished in western Europe and the British Isles under Christian leaders like Charlemagne. But the Middle Ages were also years of great conflict between Christians and Muslims in southern and eastern Europe, resulting in the Crusades—military expeditions to win the Holy Land from Muslims.

Many of the great mystics of the church lived during the Middle Ages. Monasteries and convents were a common sight across medieval Europe. Families considered themselves blessed if at least one child committed to God's service as a monk or a nun. With this lifestyle widely accepted, the best and brightest of that era entered holy orders. Monasteries and convents were the primary repository of books, so the well educated often received their training there.

We'll look at three medieval prayers that were a result of this monastic tradition.

HILDEGARD OF BINGEN: AN ECSTATIC HYMN OF PRAISE

Hildegard of Bingen lived from 1098 to 1179 in the land that became present-day Germany. She began receiving ecstatic visions from the Lord at an early age and was placed in a convent at eight years old. (*The Oxford Dictionary of the Christian Church* describes an ecstatic experience as when a person is "carried out of himself quite helplessly by some influx of special grace."[1] Paul described a similar experience in 2 Corinthians 12:1-10, which left him wondering whether he was in or out of his body. Paul's experience was accompanied by "a thorn in [his] flesh" (verse 7, NIV). Interestingly, Hildegard suffered poor health that limited her abilities to walk and see.)

She became the abbess of a Benedictine convent when she was thirty-eight and began recording her visions five years later. She wrote several books, all of which were highly influential and widespread even during her lifetime. One of those books, *Know the Ways of the Lord* (*Scivias* for short), is a record of thirteen visions about God, humanity, and heaven. She also wrote two books on medicine that show great knowledge for her day, a play, and seventy-seven pieces of polyphonic chant.

The Lord gave Hildegard a gift with language, and her visions and chants are beautiful to read. The final vision in the *Scivias* begins with a series of hymns Hildegard called the Symphony of the Blessed. She wrote that she saw a lucent sky and heard wondrous music and all the citizens of heaven singing together. They were all singing in order to give the citizens of earth the strength to resist the snares of the Devil. One of the songs she recorded them singing is this hymn of the angels who attend to God:

> *O glorious living light, which lives in Divinity!*
> *Angels who fix your eyes with ardent desire*
> *Amid the mystical darkness surrounding all creatures*
> *On Him with Whom your desires can never be sated!*
> *O glorious joy to live in your form and nature!*
> *For you are free from every deed of evil,*
> *Although that evil first appeared in your comrade,*
> *The fallen angel, who tried to soar above God,*
> *And therefore that twisted one was submerged in ruin.*

And then for himself a greater fall he prepared
By his suggestions to those whom God's hands made.

O angels with shining faces who guard the people,
O ye angels, who take just souls into Heaven,
And you, O virtues and powers, O principalities,
Dominions and thrones, who by five are secretly counted,
And you cherubim and seraphim, seal of God's secrets,
Praise be to you all, who behold the heart of the Father,
And see the Ancient of Days spring forth in the fountain,
And His inner power appear like a face from His heart.[2]

To be honest, I don't spend much of my prayer life contemplating heavenly concepts like Hildegard did. Her words are a good reminder of how magnificent and astonishing a vision of heaven can be. Revelation 4 describes such a vision. The climax of that passage offers this picture:

The Four Animals were winged, each with six wings.
They were all eyes, seeing around and within. And
they chanted night and day, never taking a break:

> *Holy, holy, holy*
> *Is God our Master, Sovereign-Strong,*
> *THE WAS, THE IS, THE COMING.* (verse 8)

Hildegard spent much of her prayer time contemplating this very scene, and her hymn is a glorious enhancement of the biblical picture. Like her, I feel that I can almost hear the music playing to a crescendo as the songs of angels and archangels, cherubim, and seraphim fill the air.

Spending some amount of our prayer time leaving behind this world and letting our spirits be lifted up into God's heavenly presence is awesome and necessary. While most of us don't receive ecstatic visions as Hildegard did, we can use her prayer to guide our spirits upward. In so doing, we can temporarily leave behind our earthly concerns and focus on our loving and intimate relationship with God through Christ.

Do you contemplate spiritual concerns when you pray? How often is heaven on your mind? How can you remind yourself to consider it more? As you read Hildegard's hymn, what images come to your mind? You might find that as you pray about heavenly concepts, your worries about this world seem less important.

FRANCIS OF ASSISI: A LIFE AND PRAYER OF GIVING

Born the son of a wealthy cloth merchant in 1181, Francis was on the path to inherit his father's business—that is, until he turned twenty. After two stints in the army, he took a pilgrimage to Rome and was deeply moved by the plight of beggars out-side Saint Peter's Basilica. He exchanged his clothes with one and spent a day begging for alms.

Changed forever by this experience, Francis returned to Assisi, left his father's business, and took up a life of poverty and service. To give you insight into his character, he once hugged a person with leprosy, a highly contagious and often-fatal skin disease, to get over his fear of it. In 1208, he took to heart Jesus' call to sell everything and follow him. Wearing a burlap sack and a rope for a belt, he set out to save souls.

As other men joined Francis, he founded the Franciscan Order; he also founded an affiliated order for women, known as the Poor Clares. The Order grew quickly as people were attracted to his simple faith in Jesus, his generosity, and his humility. Many of his prayers and sayings were collected shortly after his death. His prayer of peace is world-renowned for its beauty, and beyond that, it wonderfully captures the heart of a great saint in the history of our faith:

> *Lord, make me an instrument of your peace;*
> *Where there is hatred, let me sow love;*
> *Where there is injury, pardon;*
> *Where there is error, the truth;*

Where there is doubt, faith;
Where there is despair, hope;
Where there is darkness, light;
And where there is sadness, joy.

O Divine Master,
Grant that I may not so much seek
To be consoled, as to console;
To be understood, as to understand;
To be loved, as to love.
For it is in giving that we receive;
It is in pardoning that we are pardoned;
And it is in dying that we are born to eternal life.
Amen.[3]

This prayer sums up what should be the legacy of every Christ-follower. We should each turn the rottenness of this world upside down and inside out by being outward- and others-focused. In that way, Francis' life stands as a great example and challenge to each of us to examine our lives. Are we willing to give up everything to wholeheartedly follow Christ? Truthfully, probably not. The reason Francis' life is so exemplary was his special ability to leave everything to serve God. If many chose to do the same, his life wouldn't be such a standout.

Even if the example of his life is nearly impossible to match, we can examine our lives in light of this prayer. I can look back and ask myself whether I've sown love, pardon, truth, faith, hope, light, and joy. Would my friends, family, coworkers, and acquaintances say that I've left these virtues in my wake? We'll all fall short of the ideal, but self-examination is good for the soul. By it, we're challenged to grow in our expressions of love for God and others.

The final stanza of Francis's prayer has eternal significance to Christ-followers. While others may *say*, "It's better to give than receive," we actually believe it! We live for a faith proclaiming that life arises out of death and new life in God comes from death to self.

What kind of seeds are you sowing in your life right now? What do you want people to say about you at your funeral? What legacy do you want to leave? What might have given Francis the courage to give up everything to follow Jesus? How much courage do you need to follow Christ? Where can you get it? How can you get it?

JULIAN OF NORWICH: GOD IS ENOUGH

Very little is known of Julian of Norwich. She was born in 1342 and died sometime after 1416. At some point in her life, she had herself walled into a room attached to the church of St. Julian in Norwich, England. She saw only a handmaiden who brought her food and clean clothes.

On May 14, 1373, at the age of thirty, Julian received fifteen revelations, which she called showings, and one more revelation the next day. She wrote them down twice, immediately in a short form and some twenty years later in a longer form. Collectively they are known as the *Showings*. She had little theological training at the time she received the revelations, but her writings show a great amount of competence and literary merit.

All of the *Showings* are filled with the gentle spirit of a woman who loved Christ and wanted to know him completely. This prayer reflects her desire:

> *God, of your goodness give me yourself, for you are enough for me, and I can ask for nothing which is less which can pay you full worship. And if I ask anything which is less, I am always in want; but only in you do I have everything.*[4]

Julian must have truly wanted to be filled only with Christ and nothing else if she had herself walled into a room for her entire adult life. She gave up all the pleasures of life so she could live in continual contemplation of God.

Some of us might wonder if she had a screw loose. Believe it or not, others in medieval England also chose her lifestyle of seclusion—they're called anchorites and anchoresses, after the Greek word meaning "one who withdraws." We're fortunate that God led Julian to write down her visions so we can profit from her great sacrifice.

What do you think about Julian's example? Can you pray with her that you need nothing but God, even if you don't choose her lifestyle of seclusion? Do you sense that you have everything you need if you're filled with God? Have you ever felt that complete? What were the circumstances? Or what would it take to achieve complete fulfillment through communion with God?

CHAPTER ELEVEN

PRAYING WITH
THE MODERN CHURCH

The Western world and the church each experienced dramatic changes beginning in the sixteenth century. Society at large shifted into the Renaissance — society's reawakening to learning and the arts — and ultimately to the Enlightenment — a shift from the belief that knowledge derives from experiences to the belief that truths can be deduced by reason alone. The Enlightenment then led to the scientific and industrial revolutions. The impact of these shifts has been so great that we might feel like aliens if we were transported back to the Middle Ages.

In the church, the big change was the Reformation, during which people such as Martin Luther and John Calvin protested the corruption in the Roman Catholic Church. Although Luther hoped to reform the church from within, it didn't work out that way. Instead, many Christians followed Luther, Calvin, and others into new denominations. The Catholic Church and the new Protestant (do you recognize the word *protest* in *Protestant*?) groups ultimately benefited from this break. The church as it exists today is the result of this dramatic shift.

Christian spirituality also changed in the light of these watershed events. Protestants had a whole new way of looking at spirituality, prayer included, and Catholics, at first retrenched in the Counter-Reformation, ultimately made significant changes with the Vatican II reforms of the 1960s.

In the Protestant church, a big emphasis has always been on the unconditional grace available through Jesus Christ, so Protestant prayers often reflect this emphasis.

EVELYN UNDERHILL: A PRAYER TO SERVE

Evelyn Underhill was a great teacher of the mystical life who lived in England from 1875 to 1941. A member of the Church of England, she read widely about contemplative Christianity and drew from many sources. She taught at King's College in London, wrote many books, and was a popular retreat director.

Her teaching was especially valuable because she helped Christians realize that the contemplative life is available to anyone who desires it, not only to the so-called spiritual elite. She also showed that modern psychological theories weren't in opposition to Christian spirituality. She urged Christians to join contemplative prayer to social action, herself becoming a committed pacifist by the end of her life.

One of her prayers reads as follows:

> *O Blessed Jesus Christ, who did bid all who carry heavy burdens to come unto you, refresh us with your presence and your power. Quiet our understandings and give ease to our hearts, by bringing us close to things infinite and eternal. Open to us the mind of God, that in his light we may see light. And crown your choice of us to be your servants, by making us springs of strength and joy to all whom we serve.* [1]

This prayer is a holistic call to servanthood, a well-rounded prayer that could be used on almost any occasion, from consecrating a new day to closing a worship service. Her prayer is all about living the Christian life; the words remind us that the more we focus on the light of Christ, the better we're able to serve him wholeheartedly.

Do you need to be refreshed with God's presence and power? What changes for you when you experience his refreshment? Ask God to quiet your heart and mind so you are undistracted as you approach his throne in prayer. Have you thought about whether God may have crowned you as his choice to be a servant?

DAG HAMMARSKJÖLD: A PRAYER IN COMMUNITY WITH THE TRINITY

Dag Hammarskjöld was born in Sweden in 1905 to an overly strict father and a warm, Christian mother. A brilliant student, he progressed quickly through school and earned a Ph.D. in economics. He went to work for the government and rose in responsibility and influence, helping with the reconstruction of Europe after World War II. He was married only to his work.

In 1953, he was chosen to be the Secretary-General of the United Nations. In that post, he fought fiercely for world peace, constantly flying to world hot-spots to negotiate compromises and forge agreements. He was on such a mission in Africa on September 18, 1961, when his plane crashed in the Congo and he was killed. He won the Nobel Peace Prize posthumously.

When a friend of his was cleaning out his apartment, he found a sheaf of two-hundred neatly typed pages sitting by Dag's bedside. It turned out to be a diary he had kept for the previous thirty-six years, a diary of such profound spiritual depth that even his closest friends were shocked. Dag was known to be a gifted diplomat, but his Christianity was almost completely hidden from others.

Many of his entries are prayers, some of them hymns to God, many of them deep introspection of his own sin. One stands out above all the rest, a profound prayer to the Trinity:

> *Before Thee, Father*
> *In righteousness and humility,*
>
> *With Thee, Brother,*
> *In faith and courage,*
>
> *In Thee, Spirit,*
> *In stillness.*
>
> *Thine—for Thy will is my destiny,*
>
> *Dedicated—for my destiny is to be used and used up according to Thy will.*[2]

The power of this prayer cannot be underestimated. Even the prepositions *before, with,* and *in* have deep significance when we think of being before the Father, with the Son, and in the Holy Spirit.

Also, notice Dag's designation of Jesus as brother. Throughout his diary, which he called *Markings*, Dag wrote about his struggles with loneliness. It might not be surprising that one of the most important men of the twentieth century, jetting around the world on important missions far from friends and home for long stretches of time, struggled with lack of self-assurance and loneliness. We can only imagine that he took comfort in knowing that Christ—who also walked on this earth, who knew something about conflict, who experienced loneliness—was his brother.

To place one's destiny in God's will is a big step of humble submission for anyone, but men in power are notorious for not placing their destinies in anyone's hands but their own. Just the opposite happened with Dag, who knew putting his fate in the hands of the Triune God was the best choice he could make.

It's rare in our culture to pray to the Trinity, although we sometimes end our prayers by saying, "In the name of the Father and the Son and the Holy Spirit. Amen." Maybe we should follow Dag's example more often.

Would it seem strange to pray to Christ as your brother? Have you ever prayed to the Trinity? Try writing a prayer that addresses all three members of the Godhead.

MOTHER TERESA: A PRAYER TO SEE JESUS

Agnes Gonxha Bojaxhiu was born in 1910 in Skopje, in what is present-day Macedonia, and she joined a religious order at the age of eighteen. She spent the rest of her life, until her death in 1997, serving the poor and sick, primarily lepers in Calcutta, India. Her name is now synonymous with selflessly helping others.

She famously said that she saw Jesus in the faces of lepers, and the fearlessness with which she helped the poor and "unclean" showed that she did indeed. She made her life's goal clear: to serve Jesus. She founded the Missionaries of Charity in 1950, and in 1979 she was awarded the Nobel Peace Prize.

Mother Teresa prayed every day before beginning her work on the streets of Calcutta:

> *Dearest Lord, may I see you today and every day in the person of your sick, and whilst nursing them minister unto you.*
>
> *Though you hide yourself behind the unattractive disguise of the irritable, the exacting, the unreasonable, may I still recognize you and say: "Jesus, my patient, how sweet it is to serve you."*

Lord, give me this seeing faith, then my work will never be monotonous. I will ever find joy in humoring the fancies and gratifying the wishes of all poor sufferers.

O beloved sick, how doubly dear you are to me, when you personify Christ; and what a privilege is mine to be allowed to tend you. Sweetest Lord, make me appreciative of the dignity of my high vocation, and its many responsibilities. Never permit me to disgrace it by giving way to coldness, unkindness, or impatience.

And, O God, while you are Jesus, my patient, deign also to be to me a patient Jesus, bearing with my faults, looking only to my intention, which is to love and serve you in the person of each of your sick.

Lord, increase my faith, bless my efforts and work now and for evermore.[3]

It would be hard to imagine a prayer that better shows compassion to others. The prayer takes on added poignancy when we know that Mother Teresa's patients were dying of starvation and leprosy.

If only we all had the faith of this diminutive, hunchbacked nun who impacted the world more than any of the corporate giants of the twentieth century.

How would you change if you prayed thoughts like the ones Mother Teresa prayed every morning? What impact might you have on others? Why do we have such a hard time seeing Jesus in others, especially when they're "irritable, exacting, and unreasonable"? Is there someone in your life right now whom you'd like Jesus to make sweet to you—someone you're having a hard time loving but know you need to?

EXERCISES IN PRAYER

Now the study of prayer is over. On the following pages you'll find a selection of prayers from the past four thousand years. One—The Lord's Prayer—we looked at earlier; the others are new.

Whether they were composed three thousand years ago or thirty years ago, these prayers were all written by creations of God who wanted a more intimate relationship with their Creator. Each one is included because it has a universal, timeless quality. These prayers are here for you to *pray*, so try them.

You'll find space after each prayer for you to journal. Write down your thoughts or compose your own prayers.

When you finish with the prayer exercises in this book, these books will help you locate more prayers:

- *The Oxford Book of Prayer* by George Appleton (Oxford: Oxford, 2002). [Contains some nonChristian prayers.]

- *The Harper Collins Book of Prayers* by Robert Van de Weyer (New York: Harper Collins, 1997). [Contains some nonChristian prayers.]
- *The Doubleday Prayer Collection* by Mary Batchelor (New York: Doubleday, 1997).
- *All the Prayers of the Bible* by Herbert Lockyer (Grand Rapids, Mich.: Zondervan, 1990).

I pray that God will bless you as you walk in the footsteps of the faithful God-followers who've gone before us. They left us these signposts to lead the way.

A PILGRIM SONG

PSALM 131

The Israelites prayed this psalm on the way to the temple in Jerusalem.

GOD, I'm not trying to rule the roost,
I don't want to be king of the mountain.
I haven't meddled where I have no business
    or fantasized grandiose plans.

I've kept my feet on the ground,
    I've cultivated a quiet heart.
Like a baby content in its mother's arms,
    my soul is a baby content.

Wait, Israel, for GOD. Wait with hope.
    Hope now; hope always!

KING DAVID BLESSES THE LORD GOD

1 CHRONICLES 29:10-13

King David offered this prayer publicly as he handed the throne to his son, Solomon.

Blessed are you, GOD of Israel, our father
  from of old and forever.
To you, O GOD belong the greatness and the might,
  the glory, the victory, the majesty, the splendor;
Yes! Everything in heaven, everything on earth;
  the kingdom all yours! You've raised yourself high over
  all.
Riches and glory come from you,
  you're ruler over all;
You hold strength and power in the palm of your hand
  to build up and strengthen all.
And here we are, O God, our God, giving thanks to you,
  praising your splendid Name.

THE LORD'S PRAYER

MATTHEW 6:9-13

The prayer Jesus taught his disciples.

> *Our Father in heaven,*
> *Reveal who you are.*
> *Set the world right;*
> *Do what's best—*
> > *as above, so below.*
> *Keep us alive with three square meals.*
> *Keep us forgiven with you and forgiving others.*
> *Keep us safe from ourselves and the Devil.*
> *You're in charge!*
> *You can do anything you want!*
> *You're ablaze in beauty!*
> > *Yes. Yes. Yes.*

STEPHEN FORGIVES

ACTS 7:59-60

Stephen, the first Christ-follower to die for his faith, as he was being stoned.

> As the rocks rained down, Stephen prayed, "Master Jesus, take my life." Then he knelt down, praying loud enough for everyone to hear, "Master, don't blame them for this sin"—his last words. Then he died.

PAUL'S PRAYER TO LOVE

PHILIPPIANS 1:3-11

Paul's prayer for his friends in the church at Philippi.

Every time you cross my mind, I break out in exclamations of thanks to God. Each exclamation is a trigger to prayer. I find myself praying for you with a glad heart. I am so pleased that you have continued on in this with us, believing and proclaiming God's Message, from the day you heard it right up to the present. There has never been the slightest doubt in my mind that the God who started this great work in you would keep at it and bring it to a flourishing finish on the very day Christ Jesus appears.

It's not at all fanciful for me to think this way about you. My prayers and hopes have deep roots in reality. You have, after all, stuck with me all the way from the time I was thrown in jail, put on trial, and came out of it in one piece. All along you have experienced with me the most generous help from God. He knows how much I love and miss you these days. Sometimes I think I feel as strongly about you as Christ does!

So this is my prayer: that your love will flourish and that you will not only love much but well. Learn to love appropriately. You need to use your head and test your feelings so that your love is sincere and intelligent, not sentimental gush. Live a lover's life, circumspect and exemplary, a life Jesus will be proud of: bountiful in fruits from the soul, making Jesus Christ attractive to all, getting everyone involved in the glory and praise of God.

JUDE'S BENEDICTION

JUDE 24-25

A benediction of the New Testament church.

> *And now to him who can keep you on your feet, standing tall in his bright presence, fresh and celebrating — to our one God, our only Savior, through Jesus Christ, our Master, be glory, majesty, strength, and rule before all time, and now, and to the end of all time. Yes.*

FRANCIS OF ASSISI (1181-1226)

BROTHER SUN, SISTER MOON

A praise to the Creator of the cosmos by the founder of the Franciscans.

Most High, all-powerful, all-good Lord,
All praise is Yours, all glory, all honour and all blessings.
To You alone, Most High, do they belong,
and no mortal lips are worthy to pronounce Your Name.

Praised be You, my Lord, with all Your creatures,
especially Sir Brother Sun,
Who is the day through whom You give us light.
And he is beautiful and radiant with great splendour,
Of You Most High, he bears the likeness.

Praised be You, my Lord, through Sister Moon and the stars,
In the heavens you have made them bright, precious and fair.

Praised be You, my Lord, through Brothers Wind and Air,
And fair and stormy, all weather's moods,
by which You cherish all that You have made.

Praised be You, my Lord, through Sister Water,
So useful, humble, precious and pure.

Praised be You, my Lord, through Brother Fire,
through whom You light the night
and he is beautiful and playful and robust and strong.

Praised be You, my Lord, through our Sister, Mother Earth
who sustains and governs us,
producing varied fruits with coloured flowers and herbs.

Praise be You, my Lord, through those who grant pardon
for love of You and bear sickness and trial.
Blessed are those who endure in peace,
By You Most High, they will be crowned.

Praised be You, my Lord, through Sister Death,
from whom no-one living can escape.
Woe to those who die in mortal sin!
Blessed are they She finds doing Your Will.
No second death can do them harm.
Praise and bless my Lord and give Him thanks,
And serve Him with great humility.'

BROTHER LAWRENCE (1614-1691)

MY HEART, YOUR HEART

A Carmelite who spent most of his adult life in contemplative prayer.

> *Lord, make me according to Thy heart.*[2]

JOSEPH LOUIS BERNARDIN (1928-1996)

GRANT US MODESTY

A Roman Catholic Cardinal who promoted peace, human rights, and reconciliation.

> *Grant unto us, O Lord, the gift of modesty. When we speak, teach us to give our opinion quietly and sincerely. When we do well in work or play, give us a sense of proportion that we be neither unduly elated nor foolishly self-deprecatory. Help us in success to realize what we owe to you and to the efforts of others: in failure, to avoid dejection; and in all ways to be simple and natural, quiet in manner and lowly in thought: through Christ.* [3]

NOTES

CHAPTER 1: WHAT IS PRAYER?

1. Cited in F. L. Cross and E. A. Livingstone, eds., *The Oxford Dictionary of the Christian Church* (Oxford: Oxford, 1997), p. 1315.

CHAPTER 4: PRAYING WITH THE PSALMISTS

1. Bernhard W. Anderson, *Out of the Depths: The Psalms Speak for Us Today* (Philadelphia: Westminster Press, 1983), pp. 76-77.

CHAPTER 6: PRAYING WITH JESUS

1. This teaching is found in the *Didache*, a manual for Syrian Christians that was written about A.D. 60. Cited in Robert A. Guelich, *The Sermon on the Mount: A Foundation for Understanding* (Waco, Texas: Word, 1982), p. 284.

CHAPTER 9: PRAYING WITH THE ANCIENT CHURCH

1. George Appleton, ed., *The Oxford Book of Prayer* (Oxford: Oxford University Press, 1985), p. 74.
2. *The Book of Common Prayer According to the Use of the Episcopal Church* (New York: The Church Hymnal Corporation, 1979), p. 124.
3. Appleton, p. 106.
4. Adapted from *Service Books of the Orthodox Church, Volume I: The Divine Liturgy of St. John Chrysostom* (South Canaan, Pa.: St. Tikhon's Seminary Press, 1984), pp. 33-36.

CHAPTER 10: PRAYING WITH THE MEDIEVAL CHURCH

1. *The Oxford Dictionary of the Christian Church* (Oxford University Press, 1997), p. 528.
2. Hildegard of Bingen, *Scivias*, trans. Mother Columba Hart and Jane Bishop (New York: Paulist Press, 1990), pp. 525-526.
3. George Appleton, ed., *The Oxford Book of Prayer* (Oxford: Oxford University Press, 1985), p. 75.
4. Julian of Norwich, *Showings*, trans. Edmund Colledge, O.S.A., and James Walsh, S.J. (New York: Paulist Press, 1978), p.184.

CHAPTER 11: PRAYING WITH THE MODERN CHURCH

1. George Appleton, ed., *The Oxford Book of Prayer* (Oxford: Oxford University Press, 1985), p. 407.
2. Dag Hammarskjöld, *Markings*, trans. Leif Sjöberg and W. H. Auden (New York: Ballantine Books, 1964), p. 104.
3. Appleton, p.133.

PART 5: EXERCISES IN PRAYER

1. George Appleton, ed., *The Oxford Book of Prayer* (Oxford: Oxford University Press, 1985), p. 363.
2. Brother Lawrence, "Fourth Letter," *Practice of the Presence of God: The Best Rule of Holy Life* [online, cited 22 March 2003]; available from the World Wide Web at *http://www.ccel.org/l/lawrence/practice/htm/iv.iii.htm#iv.iv*
3. Appleton, p. 122.

BIBLIOGRAPHY

Achtemeier, Paul J., Roger S. Boraas, Michael Fishbane, Pheme Perkins, and William O. Walker Jr., eds. *HarperCollins Bible Dictionary*. Revised edition. San Francisco: Society of Biblical Literature/HarperCollins, 1996.

Anderson, Bernhard W. *Out of the Depths: The Psalms Speak to Us Today*. Philadelphia: Westminster, 1983.

Appleton, George, ed., *The Oxford Book of Prayer*. Oxford: Oxford, 1985.

Balentine, Samuel E., *Prayer in the Hebrew Bible: The Drama of Divine-Human Dialogue*. Minneapolis: Fortress Press, 1993.

The Book of Common Prayer According to the Use of the Episcopal Church. New York: The Church Hymnal Corporation, 1979.

Brother Lawrence. "Fourth Letter." Practice of the Presence of God: The Best Rule of Holy Life [online, cited 22 March 2003]. Available from the World Wide Web at *http://www.ccel.org/l/lawrence/practice/htm/iv.iii.htm#iv.iv*

Cross, F. L., and E. A. Livingstone, eds. *The Oxford Dictionary of the Christian Church*. Oxford: Oxford University Press, 1997.

Guelich, Robert A. *The Sermon on the Mount: A Foundation for Understanding*. Waco, Texas: Word Books, 1982.

Hammarskjöld, Dag. *Markings*. Translated by Leif Sjöberg and W. H. Auden. New York: Ballantine Books, 1964.

Hildegard of Bingen. *Scivias*. Translated by Mother Columba Hart and Jane Bishop. New York: Paulist Press, 1990.

Julian of Norwich. *Showings*. Translated and with an introduction by Edmund Colledge, O.S.A. and James Walsh, S.J. New York: Paulist Press, 1978.

McClendon, James W[illia]m, Jr. *Biography as Theology: How Life Stories Can Remake Today's Theology*. Philadelphia: Trinity Press, 1990.

Service Books of the Orthodox Church, Volume I: The Divine Liturgy of St. John Chrysostom. South Canaan, Pa.: St. Tikhon's Seminary Press, 1984.